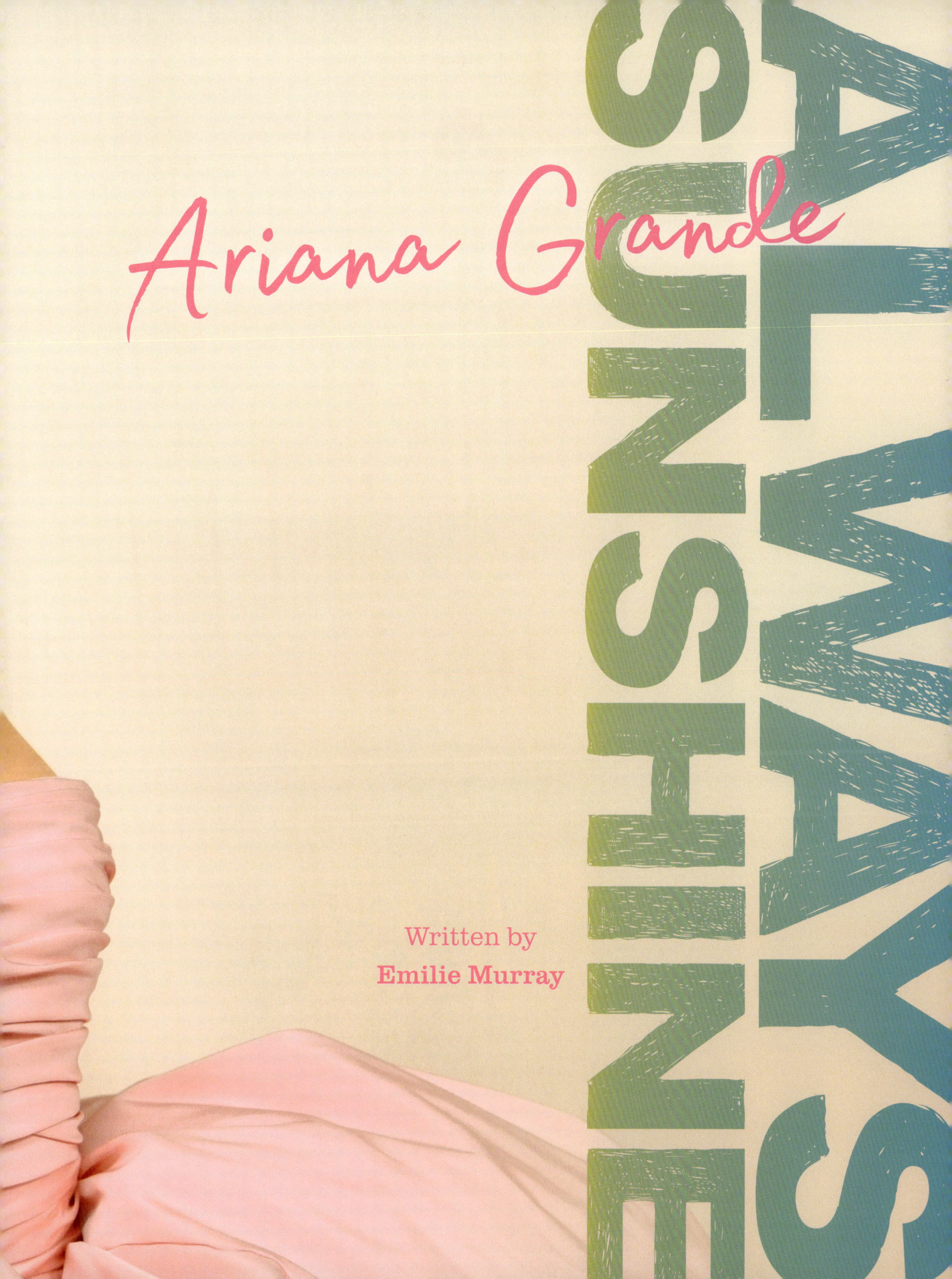

Ariana Grande

Written by
Emilie Murray

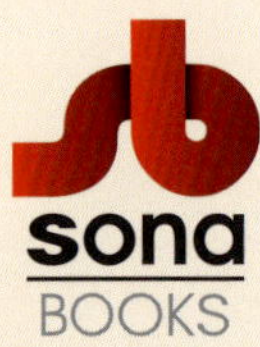

First published in the UK 2025 by Sona Books an imprint of Danann Publishing Ltd.

CAT NO: SON0658

Photography courtesy of

Getty images:

Jon Kopaloff
Thierry Orban/Sygma
Brad Barket
Jeff Kravitz/FilmMagic
Frazer Harrison
Rick Stewart /Allsport
Frank Micelotta/ImageDirect
Angela Weiss
Samir Hussein
Jason Merritt/WireImage
Ben A. Pruchnie
Kevin Winter
Jason Merritt
Flanigan/FilmMagic
Denise Truscello
Emma McIntyre
Walter McBride/Corbis
Bruce Glikas/FilmMagic
Kevin Mazur
Brill/ullstein bild
GC Images / Stringer
Jim Watson/AFP
Christopher Polk
Theo Wargo
Mike Coppola
Axelle/Bauer-Griffin/FilmMagic
Micah Smith
Steve Granitz/FilmMagic
Rich Polk/Penske Media
John Shearer/97th Oscars/The Academy

Alamy images:

dpa picture alliance
Zuma Press, Inc.
Landmark Media
Imago
PA Images
Associated Press
Album
Cinematic
Entertainment Pictures
Everett Collection Inc
TCD/Prod.DB
Gary Mather

Other images Wiki Commons

Book cover design Darren Grice at Ctrl-d
Layout design Darren Grice at Ctrl-d
Copy Editor Sofia Della Valle

Made in EU.
ISBN: 978-1-917259-23-1

CONTENTS

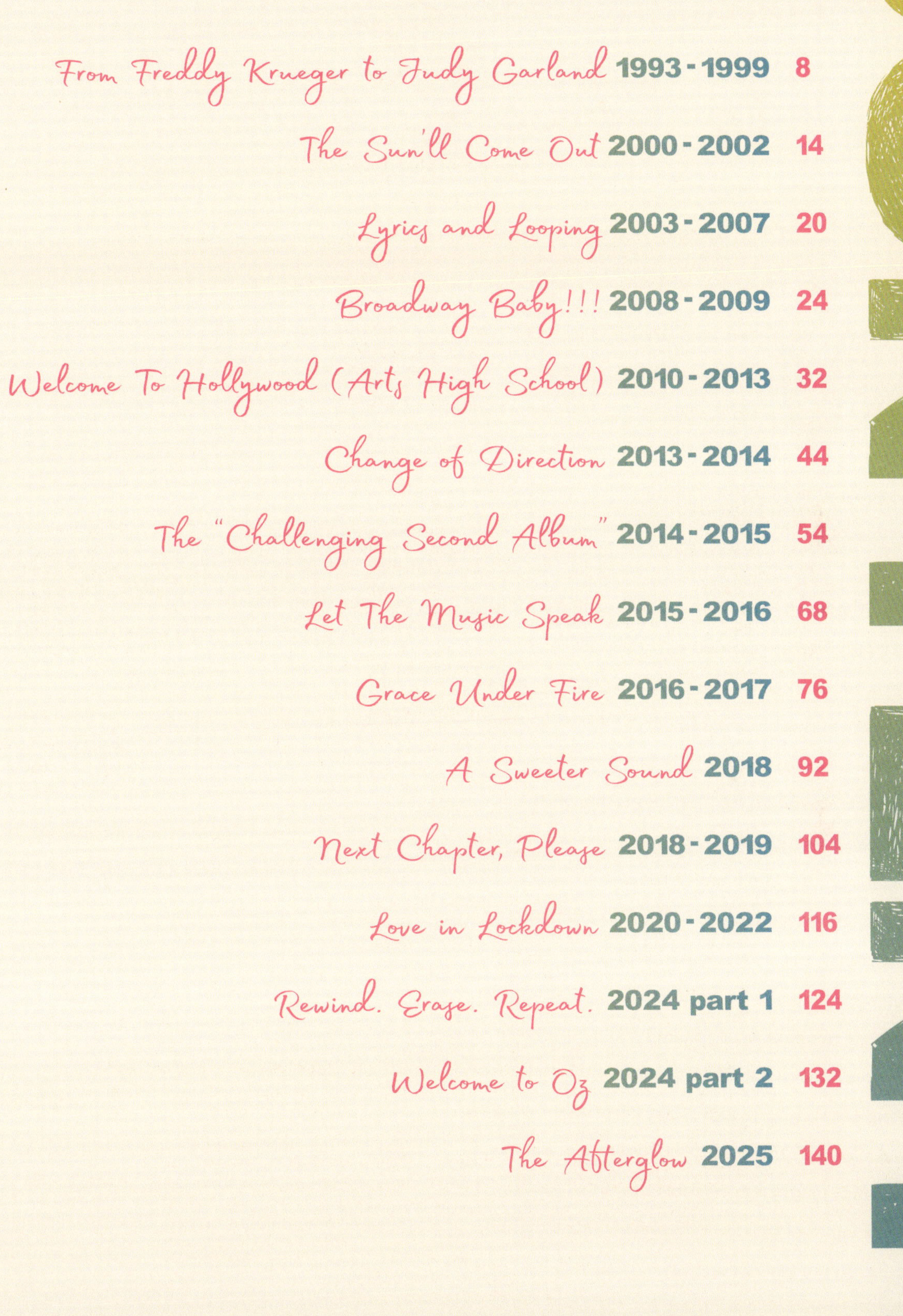

From Freddy Krueger to Judy Garland

When Joan Grande discovered she was pregnant with her second child, she couldn't have been more elated. However, nothing could have prepared her for the crazy journey she was about to embark on.

Born and raised in Brooklyn, Joan Marguerite Grande was already well acquainted with the highs and lows of motherhood. A decade before giving birth to one of the world's biggest popstars, Joan welcomed her first child, a son called Frankie, with her then-husband and pneumologist Victor Marchione, though their relationship would end shortly after. As well as being a dedicated mother, Joan built a reputation as a fiercely driven businesswoman and CEO of Hose-McCann Communications, unknowingly setting the stage to become a role model for her ambition daughter-to-be. Following her split from her first husband, Joan fell in love and married graphic designer Ed Butera. After finding out they were expecting, the couple decided to relocate with Frankie down to Boca Raton, Florida, to await their new arrival. It was in the sticky heat of the Florida summer that they welcomed their daughter, Ariana, on the 26th of June 1993. Little did Joan and Ed know that their beautiful baby girl, fittingly named after princess Oriana in *Felix and The Cat: The Movie*, would soon steal the hearts of the world one high note at a time.

But before the headlining tours, the Billboard chart-toppers, and the legions of adoring fans, Ariana was simply a bright-eyed child with an irrepressible spark. Yet, even then, this spark pointed toward something rather extraordinary about her.

Parents often have an inkling of the path their child's life might take. They will spot little hints and pick up on their kid's interests and envision how maybe all these signals will snowball into a possible future for them. And when Ariana was just a toddler, Joan realised that her daughter had quite the musical gift.

Recalling the watershed moment to *PEOPLE* magazine, Joan said, "She was probably 3, 3½, and she was in her car seat, and I was driving and listening to NSYNC as every mother should be. She hit one of JC [Chasez]'s power high notes and I kind of pulled the car over and I said, 'Ariana, was that you?'". Ariana, meanwhile, seemed completely unfazed, unaware that not every child could sing like that.

ABOVE: NSYNC

Still, Joan never expected to raise a pop star; in fact, she was briefly worried her daughter might take a darker path altogether. In a humorous anecdote Ariana once shared with *Billboard*, she revealed Joan's tongue-in-cheek suspicion that she was raising a future serial killer.

Ariana described herself as "a very weird little girl" growing up in Boca Raton. Calling herself "dark and deranged", she said, "I always wanted to have skeleton face paint on or be wearing a Freddy Krueger mask, and I would carry a hockey stick around. I was like a mini-Helena Bonham Carter". Indeed, the Grande household fostered a certain flair for the macabre.

Ariana's grandmother, Marjorie—affectionately known as Nonna—chalks this spooky streak up to their Italian roots, pointing out their love of "dark humour".

Joan, herself, is a self-described "goth before goth was goth". Famous for her signature all-black wardrobe which she acquired after a psychic told her black was her colour, Mama Grande is "the most badass, independent woman you'll ever meet", according to her daughter. But don't just take Ariana's word for it, Joan is by all accounts a hip and down to earth mother with an innate ability to connect with younger generations. She was even named by MTV as "one of the raddest moms out there".

Joan's freewheeling, verging on eccentric, parenting style exposed Ariana to grown-up culture long before

most kids even knew it existed. While her peers obsessed over caped superheroes and fairy-tale princesses, Ariana immersed herself in the raw, visceral world of body horror, fearlessly exploring themes that would send other children (and quite a few adults) running for the hills. For her fifth birthday, Ariana threw a Jaws themed birthday party, in honour of her favourite movie, where all her schoolmates promptly left crying. Reflecting on this period of her life, Ariana told *Billboard* that "it was definitely a weird phase, it went from the ages of two to about four I guess, but it was fine, and then it switched to like Dorothy outfits and healthier choices". As Ariana made way for more typical childhood pursuits, her interest in music and performance deepened exponentially. At the ripe age of just 6 years old, a pint-sized Ariana Grande decided that she was going to be a singer, and a famous one at that. "I just kind of decided that's what I'm going to do with my life, period," she recalled in an interview, "I manifested it. I knew I would. There was never really a doubt in my mind". Once she set her mind to something, there was no stopping her.

Ariana lived what most would consider to be an idyllic childhood under the heat of the Floridian sun. But even then, there was something about her quaint living room singalongs that seemed destined to turn into performances that belong on the world's biggest stages.

LEFT: Ariana's mum Joan Grande

Musical Influences

Judy Garland

Judy Garland (1922–1969) was an American singer and actress celebrated for her extraordinary vocal talent and heartfelt stage presence. Born Frances Ethel Gumm in Grand Rapids, Minnesota, she began performing in her family's vaudeville act and later signed with Metro-Goldwyn-Mayer (MGM), rising to stardom as Dorothy in *The Wizard of Oz* (1939). Her iconic performance of "Over the Rainbow" captured the hearts of viewers all over the world and cemented her place as a Hollywood icon of the Golden Age. Her resonant, emotive singing style and onstage charisma made her a role model for generations of performers, including a young Ariana, who grew up reenacting Garland's famous numbers. The pop singer has frequently spoken about her childhood admiration for Garland, saying, "every day, my mom and I would watch a different Judy Garland VHS. I love how she tells a story when she sings. It was just about her voice and the words she was singing - no strings attached or silly hair or costumes, just a woman singing her heart out. I feel like that doesn't happen that much anymore". In true Ariana fashion, she recalled first watching '*The Wizard of Oz*' as a child wearing a Dorothy inspired gingham dress paired with a '*Scream*' mask.

Whitney Houston

Whitney Houston (1963–2012) was an American singer and actress whose powerful, gospel-rooted vocals and magnetic stage presence defined a generation of pop and R&B. Born in Newark, New Jersey, to a family of accomplished singers—including her mother Cissy Houston—Whitney grew up immersed in music and began performing in church choirs. Her self-titled debut album, released in 1985, spawned multiple chart-topping singles such as "How Will I Know" and "Greatest Love of All," garnering numerous awards including several Grammys. But it was her work alongside Kevin Costner in the '*Bodyguard*' (1992), particularly her rendition of Dolly Parton's "I Will Always Love You" from the soundtrack that secured her status as a cultural phenomenon.

Ariana often cites Houston as a primary influence, emphasizing that her first real experience of wanting to be a singer was fuelled by listening to Whitney's powerful performances. "Whitney holds such a special place in my heart. She inspired me to start singing as a little girl" Ariana once shared in an interview, "I'd watch "*The Bodyguard*" and tell my mom I wanted to do that one day. Her riffs are so precise, and I love her tone. She's my inspiration". Ariana studied Houston's technique and dynamics, drawing inspiration from the way Whitney fused technical precision with raw emotion. For Ariana Grande, Whitney Houston's colossal talent and soul-stirring vocal style provided an early blueprint.

Madonna

Madonna Louise Ciccone (born August 16, 1958) is an American singer, songwriter, and cultural icon often referred to as the "Queen of Pop." Born in Bay City, Michigan, and raised in the Detroit suburbs, Madonna moved to New York City in the late 1970s to pursue a career in dance before transitioning into music. She burst onto the pop scene in the early 1980s with a string of chart-topping hits like "Holiday," "Borderline," and "Like a Virgin," swiftly gaining a reputation for her bold fashion statements, boundary-pushing performances, and knack for reinvention. Ariana grew up admiring Madonna's fearless sense of self-expression. The Material Girl's unapologetic attitude toward creativity, sexuality, and personal power made a lasting impression on the then aspiring singer. In an interview with *Cosmopolitan* in 2017, she praised Madonna's influence on her life saying, "I have the utmost respect for that woman. I love her with every ounce of my being, and not just because I'm obsessed with her entire discography. I'm so inspired by her bravery and her strength. I can look at her and not be scared to be strong". After more than four decades in the limelight, Madonna continues to reinvent what it means to be a woman in the music industry and encourage young emerging artists to forge their own paths in the pop landscape.

The Sun'll Come Out

Ariana's foray into the music world had just as much to do with acting as it did with singing. At just eight years old, she joined the Little Palm Family Theatre in Boca, which her grandparents had stepped in to save from financial trouble. It was there, under the spotlight of a humble community production, that Ariana first tasted the electric thrill of live performance. Although her mother, Joan, served on the theatre's board, Ariana's leg up compared to her peers would be of no use. When audition time came along, she would have to earn her roles based on talent alone. And that is exactly what she did. Ariana earned the coveted lead in her theatre's production of *Annie*, wowing everyone with a spirited performance.

Annie is a classic Broadway musical that follows the optimistic and feisty 11-year-old orphan Annie, who dreams of reuniting with her long-lost parents. Set during the Great Depression, the story centres on her escape from a run-down orphanage and her subsequent adventures with the wealthy Oliver "Daddy" Warbucks. Set to an iconic soundtrack, *Annie* highlights themes of hope, perseverance, and the enduring power of love to transform lives.

Ariana's performance as the titular character Annie was caught on tape and even published on the internet for everyone to see. One video in particular shows a young Ariana singing the iconic song "Tomorrow". Dressed in a tatty red dress and a curly wig, complete with fake dirt smeared all over her face, there is no denying that she looked and, more importantly, sounded the part. She hit the big notes with ease and manoeuvred the stage with the confidence of a Broadway veteran. There was little doubt, from the cast and audience members alike, that this little girl would grow up to be anything other than a star.

Ariana's love for the theatre can be directly credited to her older brother Frankie. Being a decade older than Ariana, Frankie was the subject of complete idealisation and adoration for his younger sister. Where most children would stray away from the interests of their older siblings, Ariana eagerly followed in the footsteps of her half-brother, discovering the magical world of musical theatre. Joan and Ed were equally encouraging of Ariana's extra-curricular activities. In a behind-the-scenes video of the *Annie* production the pair can be seen cheering their daughter on.

ABOVE: Ariana's brother, Frankie Grande, backstage during *Broadway Bares* at Roseland Ballroom, New York

High Notes and Hockey Pucks

Ariana made her first television debut at only eight years old when she was invited to sing the American national anthem at a Florida Panthers hockey game. In a widely circulated video clip published online, a miniature Ariana—dressed head-to-toe in black—dazzled the crowd with her rendition of "The Star-Spangled Banner", a notoriously difficult song that would challenge even the most seasoned professionals. Even the game commentators were impressed by the little girl's display of powerhouse vocals, saying "Ariana Grande-Butera, nicely done". Looking back at the footage today, the star quality radiating off Ariana was palpable, even back then.

However, that isn't the only connection the pop star has to the sport. Since the age of two, Ariana has been a massive Florida Panthers fan with her and her family attending nearly every home game.

Back in 1998, Ariana made headlines not for her music or talent as a performer, but for being hit by a puck not once, but twice at a Florida Panthers game. Ariana, then just five years old, joined by her family of proud season ticket holders took their usual seats located behind the penalty box, an area notorious for attracting stray hockey pucks. During a January 1998 game, a shot from Panthers' defenseman Gord Murphy (pictured) deflected over the glass and hit the young girl square in her right wrist. To console Ariana, the team gifted her various pieces of equipment as a consolation prize. This, as it would turn out, was not a fluke incident. Only a few months later, during a Panthers' home opener against Tampa Bay Lightning, Ariana was struck once again with a puck, securing her status as a puck magnet.

The freak accident turned even freakier when it made history. Ariana was the first fan to be hit by a puck in the Panthers' new stadium, an achievement sure to rival any of her various musical accolades.

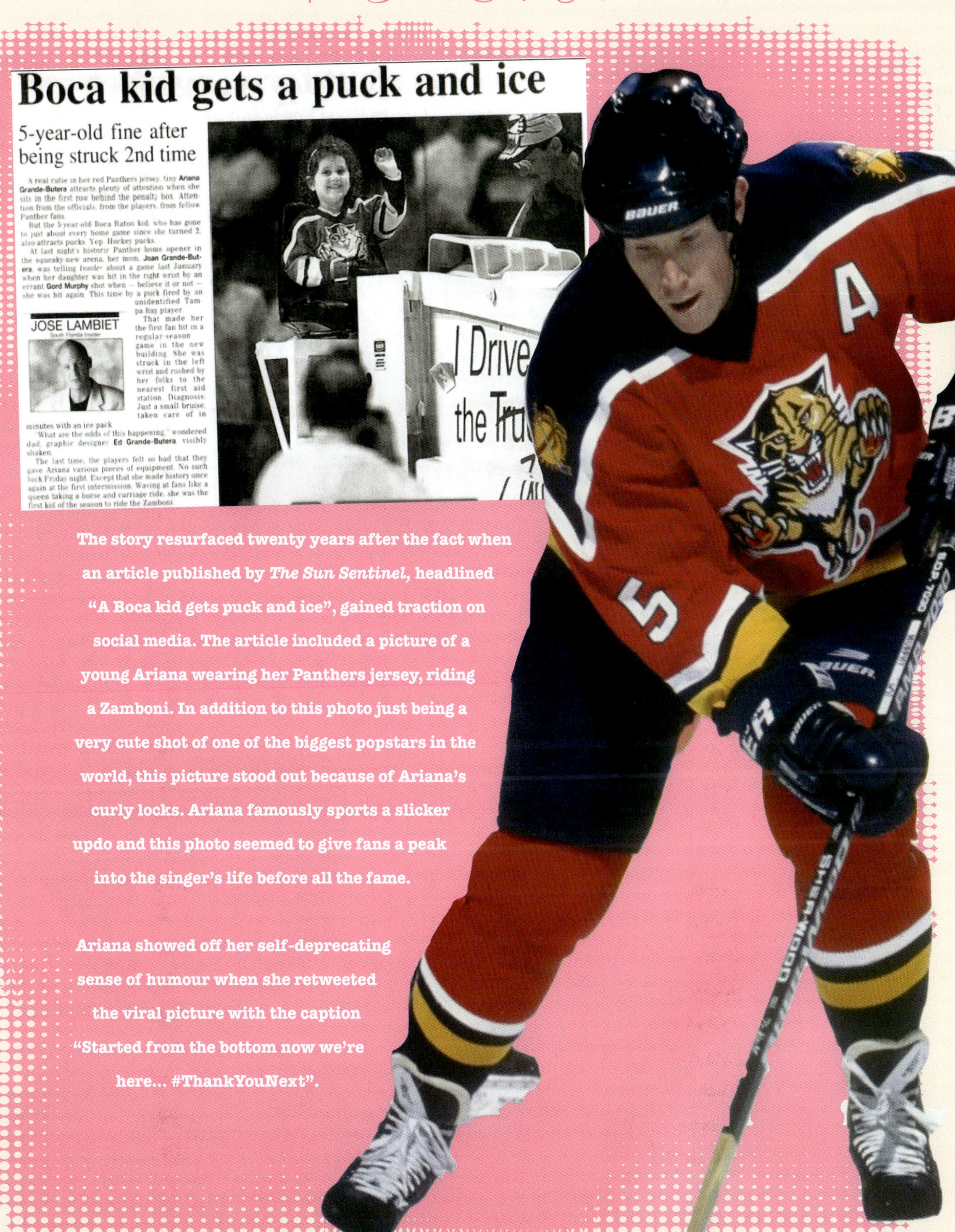

Boca kid gets a puck and ice

5-year-old fine after being struck 2nd time

A real cutie in her red Panthers jersey, tiny **Ariana Grande-Butera** attracts plenty of attention when she sits in the first row behind the penalty box. Attention from the officials, from the players, from fellow Panther fans.

But the 5-year-old Boca Raton kid, who has gone to just about every home game since she turned 2, also attracts pucks. Yep. Hockey pucks.

At last night's historic Panther home opener in the squeaky-new arena, her mom, **Joan Grande-Butera**, was telling *Insider* about a game last January when her daughter was hit in the right wrist by an errant **Gord Murphy** shot when — believe it or not — she was hit again. This time by a puck fired by an unidentified Tampa Bay player.

JOSE LAMBIET
South Florida Insider

That made her the first fan hit in a regular-season game in the new building. She was struck in the left wrist and rushed by her folks to the nearest first aid station. Diagnosis: Just a small bruise, taken care of in minutes with an ice pack.

"What are the odds of this happening," wondered dad, graphic designer **Ed Grande-Butera**, visibly shaken.

The last time, the players felt so bad that they gave Ariana various pieces of equipment. No such luck Friday night. Except that she made history once again at the first intermission. Waving at fans like a queen taking a horse and carriage ride, she was the first kid of the season to ride the Zamboni.

The story resurfaced twenty years after the fact when an article published by *The Sun Sentinel*, headlined "A Boca kid gets puck and ice", gained traction on social media. The article included a picture of a young Ariana wearing her Panthers jersey, riding a Zamboni. In addition to this photo just being a very cute shot of one of the biggest popstars in the world, this picture stood out because of Ariana's curly locks. Ariana famously sports a slicker updo and this photo seemed to give fans a peak into the singer's life before all the fame.

Ariana showed off her self-deprecating sense of humour when she retweeted the viral picture with the caption "Started from the bottom now we're here... #ThankYouNext".

Support from the Grande family was there at every turn, with her mother, Joan, always ready to drive Ariana to auditions or enrol her in dance classes if she so desired. Yet despite fostering such a nurturing environment, Joan never pushed Ariana toward a showbiz career; she merely allowed her daughter's passion to flourish on its own. When the time came to audition for *Annie*, however, Joan's protective nature went into overdrive. The theatre wouldn't let parents stay backstage unless they, too, joined the cast—so Joan jumped right in. "She had to wear a French maid's outfit and use a broom," Ariana recalled with a laugh. "She was like, 'I have no idea what I'm doing right now... but anything for my daughter.'" Although Joan was fiercely invested in her daughter's life, Ariana insists that her mother was the furthest thing away from a "stage mom", a cultural archetype of a pushy figure in a child performers life.

Ariana had found a new home in the theatre, a home that would become very dear to her heart, especially amidst the period of intense change she was about to experience. When she was just eight years old her parents announced that they would be getting a divorce. The happy family life she had previously enjoyed was slowly being ripped away from her. Ariana later commented on this time in her life and admitted how hard it was for her younger self to navigate. She told *The Sun* how she struggled to "process things" after Joan and dad Butera ended their marriage in 2001. She said: "I first saw a therapist when I was eight after my parents' divorce – but I don't think I was really mature enough to process things". Therapy would eventually become an important pillar of support for Ariana, a tool to help her deal with the highs and lows of stardom. As a result of the breakup, Ariana spent an increasing amount of time with her grandparents to escape the chaos of her household. From this point forward, Ariana and Ed's relationship would be strained and scarce, a sore spot that would later serve as inspiration for some of her biggest hits.

Everyone's Favorite
Annie jr.
"Tomorrow"
"Maybe"
"Easy Street"
"N.Y.C."
"Never Fully Dressed Without A Smile"
Introducing 8-Year-Old Ariana Grande-Butera As "Annie"
"Hard-Knock Life"
All Tickets $10
Call For Reservations
Show Times Are
Sundays, April 14,21,28 - 1pm.
At Crest Theatre, Old School Square, Delray Beach
Sundays, May 5,12,19 - 3pm. & Saturday, May 11-11am.
At The Little Theatre, Spanish River High School, Boca Raton
Call For Tickets 561.394.0206
Little Palm Family Theatre Is A Non-Profit Organization. Inquire About Our Summer Camp Little Palm 2002
Annie Jr.

RIGHT: Original poster for Ariana Grande's *Annie* performance

FAR RIGHT: Dennis Lambert

Kids Who Care

When Little Palm Theatre was forced to shut its doors, Joan and her father Frank Grande were determined to keep youth theatre alive in some way. They decided to create a children's theatre troupe called Kids Who Care and even managed to rally a small group of eight aspiring performers—including Ariana, future Broadway co-star Aaron Simon Gross, and Misha Lambert, the daughter of Grammy-nominated songwriter and producer Dennis Lambert. The Lambert family happened to be next-door neighbours with the Grande's down in Boca and their two respective girls quickly became friends through community theatre. In an interview with *Palm Beach Post* Dennis Lambert recalled that Kids Who Care often played at "black tie affairs in an effort to raise money, get exposure and be a part of a philanthropic sense of giving something back". Though small, the troupe was mighty and in 2007 alone, Ariana and her friends helped to raise over half a million dollars for charity. Dennis would occasionally participate in the do-gooding himself, having the kids do a song or two of his music or arranging a special holiday performance. Looking back on those early days, Lambert couldn't help but marvel at the talent of then 12-year-old Ariana. "She was an amazing singer," he remembers, "She could sing like Mariah Carey even back then, with that wonderful head voice, and the ability to mimic or copy all the singers she admired", before adding, "I felt, and everyone in my family felt, she was going to be a star. If not her, who?" Dennis Lambert knows what he was talking about... he produced Glen Campbell's "Rhinestone Cowboy" and co-wrote the Four Tops' "Ain't No Woman", so that kind of compliment meant he was truly faced with someone special.

By the time Kids Who Care ended, it was apparent that little Ariana, whose big voice had gotten even bigger, was intended for more than Boca children's theatre. His only piece of advice to young Ariana and her family was to "look beyond Boca".

Lyrics and Looping

Most children entertain lofty ambitions of becoming world-famous rock stars or making it big on the silver screen, but for most, those visions will always remain a fantasy. For Ariana Grande, however, music wasn't just a pipe dream—it was the only path that ever really made sense. Even as a young girl, she threw herself wholeheartedly into perfecting her craft, logging countless hours practicing her vocals, studying her idols, and taking every opportunity to perform. Rather than simply dreaming of the spotlight, Ariana treated each audition, local theatre show, or family gathering as if she were stepping onto the world's grandest stage. When she wasn't performing, she was tirelessly working on honing her talent and writing lyrics to some of her first songs. It was this relentless dedication, combined with her natural gift, that set her apart from the other children whose fanciful dreams never made it beyond their living-room stage.

The first song she ever wrote was called "Let it Rain" when she was just 12 years old. This upbeat track was released as a preview to her YouTube channel on December 7, 2008, with the description "This is a preview cut from my demo CD!" The song would eventually be cut from her self-titled demo album, but it remains on her YouTube channel for her more curious fans to check out. Though Ariana has come a long way since, going on to create some of the most enduring pop hits of the past decade, "Let it Rain" showcases a raw dedication and work ethic rarely seen in a child her age. It's a testament to the unstoppable drive that would soon take Ariana from an unknown recording booth to sold-out arenas around the globe.

Ariana has always been a great music lover. In an interview with *Complex* magazine, the young popstar discussed her musical beginnings saying, "I've always loved music. I was just always writing growing up and making cute songs with Garage Band and music was always such a massive part of my life, it's my passion". Despite an obvious infatuation with the art, Ariana never classically trained as a musician. She played the French horn for a few years, where she learned the basics of sheet music and theory, and can play a little piano, but she was never properly taught to play any instruments or even sing for that matter, preferring to teach herself through trial and error instead.

In no time at all, Ariana became a whizzkid at Garage Band, a piece of software that allows users to turn their computers, tablets or phones into a portable recording studio. Ariana also became an avid user of the looping machine, which she got one year for Christmas. A looping machine (or looper) is a piece of audio equipment, often a pedal or digital device,

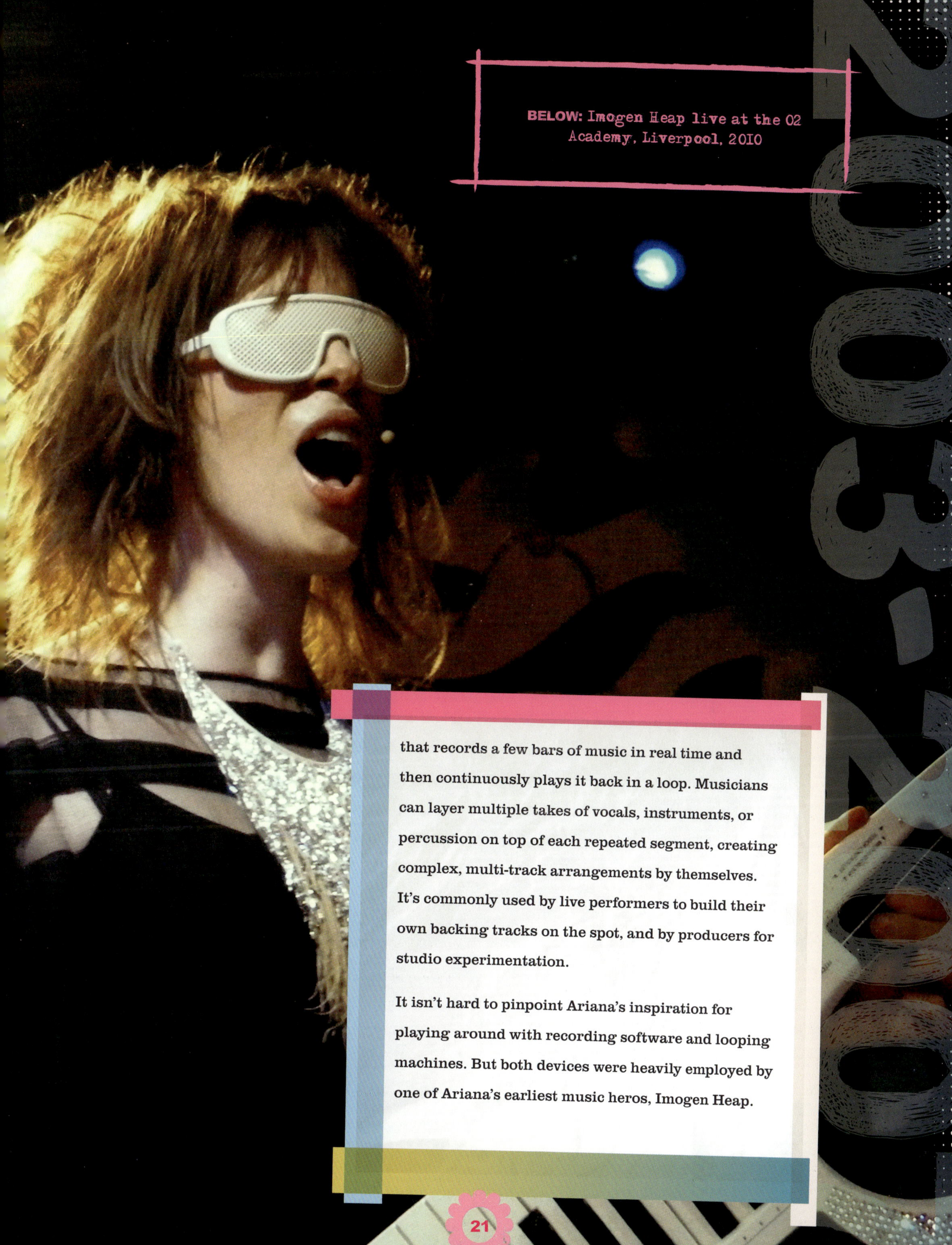

BELOW: Imogen Heap live at the O2 Academy, Liverpool, 2010

that records a few bars of music in real time and then continuously plays it back in a loop. Musicians can layer multiple takes of vocals, instruments, or percussion on top of each repeated segment, creating complex, multi-track arrangements by themselves. It's commonly used by live performers to build their own backing tracks on the spot, and by producers for studio experimentation.

It isn't hard to pinpoint Ariana's inspiration for playing around with recording software and looping machines. But both devices were heavily employed by one of Ariana's earliest music heros, Imogen Heap.

Imogen Heap

Imogen Heap, born December 9, 1977, in London, is a British singer-songwriter, record producer, and audio engineer celebrated for her inventive approach to songwriting and use of cutting-edge technology. Raised in Essex, England, Heap discovered a passion for music early on, largely teaching herself how to play instruments like the piano, clarinet, and cello, through experimentation. After attending the BRIT School for Performing Arts & Technology—a famed incubator of British talent (past alumni include Adele, Amy Winehouse and Leona Lewis)—she released her debut album titled *iMegaphone* (1998), an anagram of her own name. This record would lay the foundations for her distinctive sound, a blend of rock and experimental pop.

In 2001, Heap teamed up with producer Guy Sigsworth to form the electronic duo Frou Frou, releasing the critically acclaimed album *Details* (2002). Its lead single, "Let Go," introduced Imogen's crystalline vocals to a broader audience and showcased her love for richly layered, atmospheric production. When Frou Frou disbanded, Imogen returned to her solo career and made waves with *Speak for Yourself* (2005), an album she wrote, produced, and engineered entirely on her own. It featured "Hide and Seek," a vocoder-laced track that quickly became a pop-culture touchstone, gaining immense popularity after being featured during the climax of the season two finale of *The O.C.* The scene was later parodied in a 2007 *Saturday Night Live* digital short by comedy trio The Lonely Island called "The Shooting", which also featured the song. More recently, "Hide and Seek" was used in the soundtrack of the hit BBC and Hulu miniseries *Normal People.*

Imogen continued to explore new musical frontiers through her albums *Ellipse* (2009), recorded in her childhood home, and *Sparks* (2014), a project fuelled by fan-sourced audio. During this time, Heap began to collaborate with other high-profile artists, most notably co-writing and producing Taylor Swift's song "Clean", contributing her signature ethereal vocal layering and innovative soundscapes to the track.

Over the years, Heap has earned various accolades for her work, both

for her solo endeavours and for collaborative projects. She notably won the Grammy Award for Best Engineered Album, Non-Classical for her engineering work on *Ellipse*, making her the first female artist to ever win the award. Beyond her musical success, Imogen Heap has perhaps become most well known in recent years for her contributions to technology, as the co-developer of MiMU Gloves, a pioneering piece of wearable tech that allows musicians to shape sound through intuitive hand gestures.

Imogen's knack for merging more traditional songwriting with experimental electronics undoubtedly makes her one of the most unique artists of the 21st century. Heap's influence spans across genres, inspiring artists to explore technological innovation and vocal layering in their own work. Amid the many people inspired by Heap's music was a young Ariana Grande, who would take more than a page from her idol's handbook.

Speaking to *Billboard*, Ariana said of the "Hide and Seek" singer, "I'm absolutely her number one fan", "I appreciate her musicality so much. Her brain is a musical heaven. Every single part of each of her songs is so intricate and I just can't get enough of her". Grande recalled the first time she received a message from Imogen saying, "I thought I was being catfished", "she invited me over, and I thought I was going to be murdered because I didn't believe it was real. She was so nice. She's brilliant in every way".

The "Thank You, Next" singer has been vocal about her love of Heap for well over a decade. In 2013, Ariana shared a cover of the English musician's song "Just for Now" to her YouTube channel, with the caption "I love imogen heap with all my heart".

In her fourth studio album, *Sweetener*, Ariana covered Imogen's song "Goodnight and Go" as an homage to one of her favourite tracks from one of her favourite artists.

The pair would later get the opportunity to share the stage together, when Imogen Heap came to support Ariana during the One Love Manchester concerts.

Broadway Baby!!!

From the moment Ariana stepped onto the stage as Annie in her local Boca Raton theatre, those around her had little doubt that she was destined for anything other than stardom. But while her natural talent was undeniable from the very beginning, her big break came a little later—on a much bigger stage.

At just 15 years old, Ariana and her childhood best friend and fellow Kids Who Care bandmate Aaron Simon Gross, took a massive leap of faith and travelled to New York City to audition for a brand-new musical opening on Broadway. It was a long shot, with thousands of likeminded young performers vying for a spot in the production. Yet, against all odds, both Boca Raton natives landed parts in the show, with Ariana as Charlotte, a popular cheerleader, and Aaron as Archie, a boy with muscular dystrophy. "I auditioned for 13, and out of thousands of kids, they picked me," Ariana recalled in an interview with *Complex* magazine. "I was so blessed. I came to New York with my best friend, and we grew up together doing musical theatre since we were like seven years old. We both got it, out of thousands of kids. It was insane. The cast was 13 kids, and out of 13 kids, we made it. How is that even possible?"

13: The Musical premiered on Broadway at the Bernard B. Jacobs Theatre on October 5, 2008, and ran until January of the following year. Though its Broadway run was relatively short-lived, the show became somewhat of a cultural touchstone for all the theatre-loving teens of the late 2000s. *13* came about at a pivotal time in pop culture. Broadway was still reeling from the success of *Spring Awakening* (2006), a daring, boundary-pushing musical about teenage self-discovery that won the Tony Award for Best Musical in 2007. Meanwhile, outside of Broadway, *High School Musical,* released in 2006, had exploded into a global sensation proving that there was an enormous appetite for coming-of-age stories that authentically captured the teenage experience. For the first time, young audiences were recognized as a powerful market that needed catering to.

But what truly set *13* apart, was its groundbreaking place in Broadway history. It was the first musical ever to feature an all-teen cast and band, with most of the performers under the age of 15. From the leads to the ensemble to the musicians in the pit, every aspect of the show was powered by teenagers, making it unlike any other Broadway production about adolescence, usually performed by adults or older teens. *13* offered a new level of authenticity as it depicted middle school life played by actors who were living through it. It was a musical about kids, for kids, and most importantly, performed by kids—offering audiences a refreshingly real portrayal of the awkward and often deeply funny moments that accompany the preteen years.

MAIN IMAGE: Ariana at the curtain call following the opening performance of 13 at the Bernard B. Jacobs Theatre in New York City, October 5, 2008

The Plot

13 is a coming-of-age musical that follows Evan Goldman, a 12-year-old boy from New York City, whose life is turned upside down when his parents get divorced. Forced to leave his friends and fast-paced city life behind, Evan moves with his mother to a small town in Indiana, just as he's preparing for his Bar Mitzvah. Determined to make new friends and solidify his social status, he sets his sights on the popular crowd, particularly Brett, the school's star quarterback, and his friends Malcolm and Eddie.

In his attempt to fit in, Evan distances himself from the nerdier kids, including Patrice, an intelligent and kind-hearted girl who genuinely wants to be his friend, and Archie, a witty and sarcastic classmate with muscular dystrophy. As Evan navigates the complexities of middle school drama—including first crushes, peer pressure, and social cliques—he realizes that popularity isn't as important as true friendship.

MAIN IMAGE: Ariana, Brynn Williams, Jason Robert Brown, and company taking in the applause following the opening performance of 13 at the Bernard B. Jacobs Theatre in New York City, October, 2008

The involvement of musical theatre rockstar and three-time Tony recipient, Jason Robert Brown in the show, only added to the buzz surrounding the project. The then 38-year-old Broadway prodigy had a string of successful musicals under his belt, and both critics and theatre nerds alike were eager to see his latest piece of work. Brown was the composer for *13,* writing all the music and lyrics, and 15 years after the musical's Broadway debut, Jason sat down with *Grammy.com* to reminisce about his experience making the show and the talent that it subsequently produced. "She sang Mariah Carey" said Brown recalling Ariana's audition, "She opened her mouth, and we said, 'we have cast her'. "She was always an extraordinarily talented creature. So many of those kids in that original company were".

Jason went on to say that in the opening number of the original cast album, the series of four solo riffs at the end of the song were entirely improvised by the children. He recalled gathering all 13 cast members around the piano, repeatedly playing the same four measures of music while encouraging each child to create their own riff when he pointed to them. "I got to Ariana, and she sang this sort of perfect Whitney Houston riff right at the end of the song. It was amazing. What I remember specifically as she sang it was everybody just started laughing because we were all like well, we can stop doing this now. We know what one of the riffs is going to be". Despite giving Ariana her first professional singing gig, Jason doesn't like to take credit for the popstar's immense success, even if he did play a hand in it. "She

was going to be famous no matter what happened" he explained, "I do feel like we got to give her this little showcase where the world got to see her for the first time".

Ariana is undoubtedly the most well-known of her former *13* cast members, however, there's no denying that the musical served as a launchpad for more than one talented performer.

MAIN IMAGE: Ariana performing on stage as Charlotte in 13 at the Bernard B. Jacobs Theatre in New York City, October 5, 2008

Broadway Stars

Liz Gillies

Elizabeth "Liz" Gillies (born July 26, 1993) is an American actress, singer, and songwriter. She began her career in commercials before making her Broadway debut in *13: The Musical*, where she met Ariana Grande, forming a lifelong friendship. Gillies rose to fame as Jade West in *Victorious* (2010–2013), starring alongside Grande, and quickly became a fan favourite for her dark humour and strong vocals. After *Victorious*, she continued her acting career with roles in *Sex & Drugs & Rock & Roll* (2015–2016) and later starred as Fallon Carrington in *Dynasty* (2017–2022), The CW's modern reboot of the classic soap opera. Beyond acting, she has collaborated multiple times with Seth MacFarlane, lending her voice to characters in *Family Guy* and *American Dad* and performing jazz duets with him on various projects. Gillies has also frequently worked with Ariana Grande, joining her onstage for live performances and making appearances in her music projects. Their enduring friendship remains a core part of both their personal and professional lives, with Ariana often referring to Liz as one of her closest friends.

Tinashe

Tinashe Jorgensen Kachingwe (born February 6, 1993) is an American actress, dancer, songwriter and singer, known for her genre-blending music and electrifying stage presence. Born in Lexington, Kentucky, and raised in Los Angeles, Tinashe began her career as a child actress, landing roles in films like *Akeelah and the Bee* (2006) and TV shows such as *Two and a Half Men*. Before rising to fame as a solo artist, Tinashe was part of the original workshop cast of *13: The Musical*, where she helped develop the show before it made its way to Broadway. Following her time in musical theatre, Tinashe shifted her focus to music, eventually launching a successful R&B/pop career with hits like "2 On" and "All Hands-on Deck." Her background in acting and theatre has continued to influence her artistry, blending storytelling with her signature futuristic sound and dynamic performances.

Graham Phillips

Graham Phillips (born April 14, 1993) is an American actor, singer, and director known for his work in television, film, and theatre. Born in Laguna Beach, California, he began his career at a young age, making his Broadway debut as the lead, Evan Goldman, in *13*. He worked alongside Ariana and the pair would quickly strike up a romantic relationship. The young couple dated for a few years after meeting in *13* but eventually split up around 2011. Despite their breakup, they have remained on good terms over the years, occasionally reuniting for friendly get-togethers. Following *13*, Phillips gained widespread recognition for his role as Zach Florrick in *The Good Wife* (2009–2016), where he played the son of Julianna Margulies' character. He has also appeared in films like *Evan Almighty* (2007) and *Blockers* (2018) and took on the role of Prince Eric in ABC's *The Little Mermaid Live!* (2019).

Welcome To Hollywood
(Arts High School)

After dazzling audiences on Broadway, Ariana was ready for the next big leap in her career—transitioning from the big stage to the small screen. For decades, television had been the launching pad for numerous successful careers, with Disney Channel in particular, serving as a powerful springboard for young talent who would later go on to dominate the worlds of music, film, and television. The legendary Mickey Mouse Club paved the way for icons like Justin Timberlake, Britney Spears, Christina Aguilera, and Ryan Gosling, each of whom parlayed their early exposure into wildly successful runs in showbusiness. The channel also introduced audiences to Miley Cyrus and Selena Gomez, performers who have grown into international superstars with impressive portfolios spanning multiple entertainment genres. More recently, Nickelodeon started to cultivate its own stable of rising talent, with breakout stars like Miranda Cosgrove and Amanda Bynes captivating audiences and becoming household names. Together, these networks have not only entertained millions but also provided a platform for generations of remarkable performers to transform their early dreams into lasting, multifaceted careers.

Ariana got her big break when she landed the role of Cat Valentine on Nickelodeon's new TV show *Victorious,* alongside her former *13* co-star and best friend Liz Gillies. Unlike the meticulously rehearsed environment of musical theatre, television offered a new, more spontaneous arena where Ariana could really let her playful spirit shine. But more importantly, the show would expose Ariana to a much wider audience, placing her in the living rooms of hundreds of thousands, sometimes millions, of viewers every week. "I didn't do any other musical theatre after 13, and then I went to L.A. and I auditioned for Victorious", the popstar later recalled, "I loved Nickelodeon growing up and I wanted to audition for a Nickelodeon show as soon as I found out that they were doing them. I think that Cat is a role that I was meant to play. There are roles that people are just right for, and I think Cat is mine".

MAIN IMAGE: Ariana performing live at the IPOP Concert Series: An Evening with the Make-A-Wish Foundation and Starlight Children's Foundation, held in Los Angeles on January 9, 2010

ABOVE: Ariana Grande as Cat Valentine

RIGHT: (L R) Elizabeth Gillies, Daniella Monet, Victoria Justice, Avan Jogia, Matt Bennett, Leon Thomas III, and Ariana Grande cast of Victorious at Nickelodeon's 2011 Kids' Choice Awards at the Galen Center in Los Angeles, 2011

The Plot

Victorious is a situational comedy series that follows Tori Vega (Victoria Justice), a talented teenager who enrols in Hollywood Arts High School—a prestigious performing arts school where creativity meets chaos. Tori and her eclectic group of friends, including musical prodigy Andre Harris (Leon Thomas III), the socially awkward Robbie Shapiro (Matt Bennett) and the sweet yet dim-witted redhead Cat Valentine (Ariana Grande) learn to navigate the ups and downs of adolescence. Also wandering the halls of Hollywood Arts is Jade West (Elizabeth Gillies), the sarcastic and sometimes antagonistic peer who serves as Tori's frenemy, along with her down-to-earth, handsome actor boyfriend, Beck Oliver (Avan Jogia), and Tori's self-absorbed, less-talented older sister, Trina (Danielle Monet). The odd bunch of teenagers tackle everything from quirky class assignments and artistic rivalries to the challenges of balancing school life with the pursuit of stardom. With each episode packed with catchy musical numbers and humorous mishaps, the show captures the energy, passion, and resilience of young performers as they learn to overcome obstacles and chase their dreams in the spotlight.

On its debut in March 2010, *Victorious* was watched by 5.7 million people, making it Nickelodeon's second highest premier for a live action show after *Big Time Rush*.

Ariana's portrayal of Cat Valentine on *Victorious* quickly became one of the show's most defining elements, thanks in large part to the character's instantly recognizable look and quirky charm. One of Cat's most striking features was her bright red hair, a detail the creator of the show, Dan Schneider, suggested himself. 'It was totally genius, and I can't see my character any other way" Ariana said about playing her character, "We did a flashback episode, and even young she had it. She made this decision early and it became part of her. And I have to thank Dan because it helps me play her. When I dyed my hair, it gave me a new energy that I could bring into the character".

BELOW: Dan Schneider

BOTTOM LEFT: Ariana Grande poses on the set of *Victorious* in Hollywood, California on February 22, 2011

Dan Schneider

Dan Schneider (born January 14, 1966) is an American television producer, screenwriter, and actor best known for creating and producing some of Nickelodeon's most iconic shows.

Born and raised in Memphis, Tennessee, Schneider briefly attended Harvard University before returning to his hometown to work in computer repair. However, his passion for entertainment soon led him to Los Angeles, where he pursued a career in acting. In the 1980s, he appeared in several comedy movies, including *Better Off Dead* (1985) with John Cusack, and *The Big Picture* (1989), starring Kevin Bacon. He landed a recurring role on ABC's television sitcom *Head of the Class* which ran for a total of 5 seasons from 1986 and 1991. While working in television, Schneider developed an interest in writing and producing. His big break came when he co-created the hit Nickelodeon sketch comedy show *All That* (1994–2005), which became a massive success and launched the careers of stars like Kenan Thompson and Amanda Bynes. This success led him to create *The Amanda Show* (1999–2002), further solidifying his role as Nickelodeon's go-to creator for teen and tween entertainment. Some of his other hit shows include *Drake and Josh* (2004-2007), *Zoey* 101 (2005-2008), *iCarly* (2007-2012), *Victorious* (2010-2013) and *Sam & Cat* (2013-2014).

Despite his success, Schneider's time at Nickelodeon ended controversially in 2018 when he and the network parted ways following allegations of a toxic work environment. While no formal charges were made, reports surfaced regarding inappropriate workplace behaviour and on-set treatment of young actors. Since then, Schneider has remained largely out of the public eye, though he has hinted at future projects.

Stellar Singles

Give It Up

"Give It Up" made its debut on the Nickelodeon sitcom *Victorious* during a one-hour special titled "Freak the Freak Out," which aired on November 26, 2010. In this episode, Tori Vega and her friends attend a weekly singing contest at Karaoke Dokie, a fictional karaoke bar, where Jade West and Cat Valentine team up to perform the catchy track. The song was later officially released as the seventh track on the show's debut soundtrack album, *Victorious: Music from the Hit TV Show*, on August 2, 2011, marking the musical debuts of both Liz Gillies and Ariana Grande. Written by producer Dan Schneider, Michael Corcoran, and CJ Abraham, "Give It Up" also made a splash on the charts, debuting and peaking at number 23 on the US Billboard Bubbling Under Hot 100 chart in August 2011.

Fast forward to November 2019: after resuming her Sweetener World Tour following a brief illness-induced hiatus, Ariana teased a special project on Twitter, writing, "Guys I can't tell u why yet, but I'm so excited for tonight. I've never felt this way. Goodbye." Later that night at a concert in Atlanta, she surprised fans by inviting Liz onstage to perform a nostalgic rendition of "Give It Up" together.

MAIN IMAGE: Ariana live onstage during the IPOP Concert Series: An Evening with the Make-A-Wish Foundation and Starlight Children's Foundation in Los Angeles on January 9, 2010

G-STAR
ORIGINALS
VARIETY

The release of "Give It Up" proved to be a watershed moment for Ariana, as it gave her the confidence she needed to take her talent beyond television and pursue her true passion: music. Energised and inspired by the track's success, she began uploading covers of her favourite songs onto her YouTube channel, recording them in makeshift sound setups in her bedroom. Despite the humble beginnings, Ariana's innate talent shone through and quickly captured the attention of fans and industry insiders alike. At the time, YouTube was just starting to revolutionize the music industry as it allowed aspiring artists to showcase their skills directly to a global audience, bypassing traditional gatekeepers. For record label executives, the platform made it easier than ever to scout emerging talent. A prime example of a YouTube success story is none other than the discovery of Justin Bieber, whose early covers posted to the platform paved the way for his meteoric rise to fame. Though Ariana already had a following through her work on *Victorious*, it was her YouTube channel that caught the eyes of music industry executives. A friend of Monte Lipman, the chairman of Republic Records, saw one of her videos and sent it to the industry giant. This exposure led to the release of her first official single, "Put Your Hearts Up", in December 2011.

Although the track played a crucial role in launching her career, Ariana has since distanced herself from it, feeling that its bubble gum pop sound was tailored too much for her young *Victorious* fanbase and didn't align with the mature artistic identity she wanted to embody. Despite this, "Put Your Hearts Up" remains an important milestone in the evolution of a star who would go on to redefine pop music on her own terms.

RIGHT: Monte Lipman

LEFT: Justin Bieber and Ariana Grande attend Variety's 4th Annual Power of Youth event at Paramount Studios in Hollywood, California, on October 24, 2010

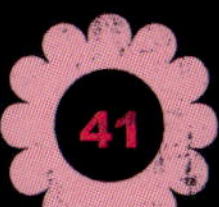

Drama Queens

Victorious had a cast packed with incredible talent, but this abundance of big personalities sometimes clashed and sparked some off-screen drama. Rumours of a feud between Ariana Grande and Victoria Justice first began circulating in April 2010. During an on-set interview with *Popstar! Magazine*, the girls of the *Victorious* cast—including Ariana, Victoria, Elizabeth Gillies, and Daniella Monet—playfully revealed their cast secrets. What started as a light-hearted exchange quickly sparked speculation about tension between the two stars. In the now-famous clip, Liz talked about Ariana's tendency to sing a lot. "She sings everything," Liz said. "And it's a good thing because she has a beautiful voice, but it's awesome. She sings absolutely everything, she never stops". Daniella then chimed in to say that Liz also sings a lot, which prompted Victoria to say, "I think we ALL sing". The moment didn't seem like anything but an awkward interview at the time, but Victoria's response was later interpreted by fans as a passive-aggressive dig at Ariana, fuelling speculation of an off-screen rift.

The rumours only intensified when Nickelodeon announced that *Victorious* would not be returning for a fourth season. Fans were quick to speculate that Ariana was to blame, particularly since she had just landed a role on *Sam & Cat* alongside Jennette McCurdy. Frustrated by the accusations, Ariana took to *ask.fm* to set the record straight, clapping back at a fan saying, "Sweetheart, the only reason *Victorious* ended is because one girl didn't want to do it," she wrote. "She chose to do a solo tour instead of a cast tour. If we had done a cast tour, Nickelodeon would have ordered another season of *Victorious* while *Sam & Cat* filmed simultaneously, but she chose otherwise. I'm sick of this BS". Many assumed Ariana was referring to Victoria, who had embarked on her Summer Break Tour in 2013.

While Victoria never directly addressed Ariana's comments, she did post a cryptic tweet shortly after that many believed was aimed at her former co-star. "Some people would throw some1 that they consider a friend under the bus just 2 make themselves look good. #StopBeingAPhony #IfTheyOnlyKnew." The tweet only added more fuel to the fire and seemingly confirmed the alleged rift between two of the biggest stars on Nickelodeon's most talked-about show.

The rumour mill went into overdrive yet again, this time it was when Ariana sat down with *Seventeen* for her June 2013 cover story interview and discussed some drama with a former unnamed co-star. "I worked with someone who told me they'd never like me," she said. "But for some reason, I just felt like I needed her approval. So, I started changing myself to please her. It made me stop being social and friendly. I was so unhappy". As always, the internet jumped to the conclusion that Ariana must be talking about her former *Victorious* co-star, Victoria. Despite both women repeatedly coming out and shutting down the rumours, speculation about a feud between them refused to fade, even years after the show's end.

In 2015, Victoria responded to Ariana's quote on *The Meredith Vieira Show*. "I would love to set the record straight because

I feel like these rumours have been going on for way too long," she said. "So, basically there was an article in Seventeen magazine where she had said that she was bullied on set and the magazine basically alluded to it being me. So, once the article came out — actually before it came out — she texted me privately and was like, 'Oh my gosh. I am so sorry, you know how the media twists words. I was not talking about you, obviously. I was talking about someone on Broadway that I had worked with". Despite Victoria clearly denying any beef between herself and the popstar, eagle-eyed fans were quick to spot that she did not appear in Ariana's 2018 music video for her song "Thank You, Next" even though Liz Gillies, Daniella Monet and Matt Bennett all made surprise cameos in the clip.

Over the years Ariana has also tried to squash rumours of feud. Recently, in honour of *Victorious'* 10th anniversary, the stars took to Instagram to share old pics and memories from their time on the show. Of course, old memories brought up old feud rumours, and one fan commented on Ariana's Instagram, "I think we're ALL the best". To which Ariana cooly responded with "Shut the f*ck up", effectively ending the conversation right then and there.

At the end of the day, the rumoured feud between Ariana and Victoria seems to have been nothing more than internet-fuelled speculation, with little real substance behind it. Both women have gone on to thrive in their respective careers, Ariana as a global pop sensation and Victoria as a successful actress and singer. Though, this would not be the last time Ariana would be labelled a "Drama Queen". Just a year after the end of *Victorious,* the popstar made headlines yet again, when she seemingly became embroiled in a feud with her *Sam & Cat* co-star Jennette McCurdy.

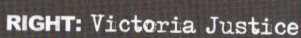

RIGHT: Victoria Justice

Change of Direction

Despite the cancellation of *Victorious* in 2013, Ariana Grande quickly stepped back into her iconic role as Cat Valentine for Nickelodeon's new spin-off series, *Sam & Cat*. Created by Dan Schneider, the mastermind behind both *Victorious* and *iCarly*, the show brought together two beloved characters in a fun crossover designed to capitalize on the popularity of both series. *Sam & Cat* paired the tough, sarcastic Sam Puckett (played by Jennette McCurdy) with the quirky, bubbly, and sometimes naive Cat Valentine (played by Ariana Grande). The stark contrast between their personalities became a key element of the show, fuelling its comedic tone and keeping viewers engaged.

The Plot

After Carly Shay moves to Italy with her father, Sam Puckett embarks on a West Coast motorcycle tour, eventually landing in Venice, Los Angeles. There, fate intervenes when Sam spots the quirky Cat Valentine being unceremoniously tossed into the back of a garbage truck, prompting her to rescue the spirited redhead. The two quickly forge a deep bond and become roommates, setting the stage for a series of wild, unpredictable adventures. Deciding to forgo traditional after-school jobs, the two girls decide to launch an unconventional babysitting service instead, aptly calling it "Sam and Cat's Super Rockin' Fun-Time Babysitting Service". Their zany business venture hurls them into a string of humorous mishaps alongside a crew of eccentric characters, including their money-minded neighbour Dice, the dim-witted MMA fighter Goomer managed by Dice, and Nona, all of whom add to the chaotic charm of their world.

TOP RIGHT: Jennette McCurdy and Ariana Grande attend the UK premiere of *Sam & Cat* in London, October 2013

RIGHT: Promo shot for *Sam and Cat*

Production for *Sam & Cat* began on a 20-episode order in January 2013 and premiered June 8, with the pilot episode garnering a total of 4.16 million viewers, making it yet another runaway hit for the network. Several weeks later, on July 11, Nickelodeon doubled the season one order of 20 episodes, to 40, following the high ratings of the show. However, by September, as filming resumed for the second half of the season, Ariana found herself at a crossroads.

While she had spent years building a strong fanbase through her role as Cat Valentine on *Victorious* and *Sam & Cat,* she was now determined to establish herself as a serious musician in her own right. At first, Ariana embraced her role with enthusiasm, revelling in Cat's offbeat humour and whimsical innocence. However, as Ariana's career evolved and her artistic ambitions grew, the initial connection she felt towards Cat Valentine began to wane. Although Cat was conceived as a light-hearted, comedic figure—intentionally designed to be endearingly dim-witted—the one-dimensional portrayal eventually felt restrictive to the aspiring popstar. Critics often panned the character for her lack of depth, suggesting that the humour derived from Cat's naive simplicity overshadowed the rich talent that Ariana possessed. As the singer began gearing up to release her debut album, she also sought to distance herself from her Nickelodeon persona to explore more mature and diverse facets of her artistry.

Ariana Grande's debut album, *Yours Truly*, was released on September 3, 2013, marking a definitive shift in her career from television star to a serious musical artist. The album was an immediate success, debuting at No. 1 on the US Billboard 200 chart and selling over 138,000 copies in its first week. The record was initially praised for its retro 90s R&B style, highlighting Ariana's impressive vocal range with many critics likening the new popstar to Mariah Carey.

Stellar Singles

Honeymoon Avenue

The album opens with the smooth, nostalgic "Honeymoon Avenue", which sets the tone for *Yours Truly* with its jazzy, old-school vibes. The song's lush, orchestral arrangement gives it a timeless feel, while Ariana's powerful voice takes centre stage. Lyrically, "Honeymoon Avenue" deals with the complexities of a relationship that has lost its initial spark yet still holds hope for rekindling the romance. Ariana's voice is emotive and vulnerable, proving her ability to convey emotion while still sounding effortlessly controlled.

The Way

"The Way" was the album's lead single and quickly became one of Ariana's first breakout hits. Featuring Mac Miller, the song combines pop and R&B sounds, showcasing Ariana's ability to balance breathy and sultry vocals with powerhouse deliveries. The song is also notable for its use of the sample from the 1970 hit "I've Got a Woman" by The Impressions. While promoting "The Way", Ariana discussed the inspiration behind the

RIGHT: Her first album *Yours Truly*
BELOW: Ariana in 2013

track saying, "it's about loving somebody so much you can't take it. The early stages of being in love and how exciting it is and how much it drives you crazy and how amazing it feels". Ariana's voice is light and airy, perfectly conveying the carefree and playful and euphoric feeling of having a crush. The lyrics are simple, but they feel universal, which is part of what makes the song so relatable to wider audience. In addition to the song's great production and lyricism, it was the chemistry between Ariana and Mac Miller that really cemented "The Way" as one of

the biggest bops of 2013. Their playful back-and-forth in the chorus and the verses added a layer of charm to the track, making it feel like an effortless, natural collaboration.

It also marked the beginning of an important relationship for the singer, both in her personal and professional life. Ariana's friendship with Mac only continued to blossom after the recording of their duet and would even turn romantic a few years after the release of "My Way".

The song debuted at number 10 on the Billboard Hot 100 and remained in the Top 10 for several weeks, eventually peaking at number nine. It was certified Platinum by the RIAA and became one of the defining songs of 2013.

LEFT: Mac Miller

Almost Is Never Enough

"Almost Is Never Enough" featuring Nathan Sykes is a soulful ballad about the bittersweet feeling of being close to making a relationship work but ultimately falling short. The song features an orchestral pop production, with a gentle piano intro and strings that build into an emotional crescendo. Ariana and Nathan's vocals complement each other beautifully, with Ariana's powerful voice blending perfectly with Nathan's smooth tenor. Lyrically, the song explores the idea that, despite deep feelings, love isn't always enough to overcome obstacles. A shortened version of "Almost Is Never Enough" is also included on the official soundtrack for the 2013 fantasy film *The Mortal Instruments: City of Bones.*

The chemistry and heartfelt performances between Ariana and Nathan make this duet a standout track on *Yours Truly*, which isn't surprising considering the pair entered into a romantic relationship shortly after recording the track.

Music, Romance and Headlines

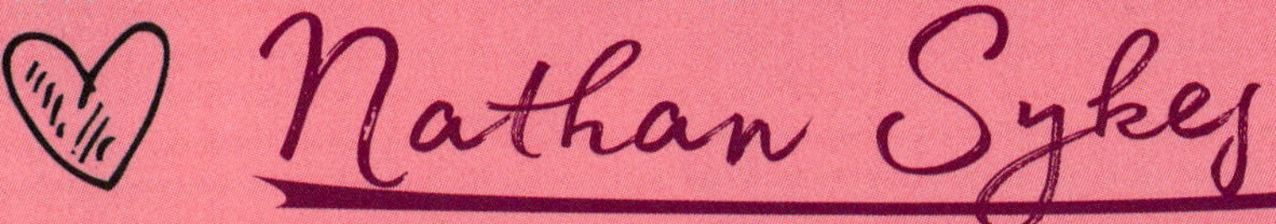

Nathan Sykes

Ariana Grande and Nathan Sykes, a member of the British boy band The Wanted, were first romantically linked in August 2013 after they recorded the duet "Almost Is Never Enough" for Ariana's debut album *Yours Truly*. Their romance, however, sparked controversy when Ariana's ex-boyfriend, Australian comedian Jai, accused her of cheating on him with Nathan, a claim she vehemently denied. Ariana hit back on Twitter, writing: "I guess I shouldn't be so surprised. You said to me if I didn't come back to you, you'd make me look bad to the entire world... I'm no longer afraid of you or your lies anymore." Despite the drama, Ariana and Nathan were spotted together several times, including a dinner date in London in early November and in late August in New York City. Though their romantic relationship was brief, it marked an important chapter in Ariana's early career, both inside and outside of work. The pair are also said to have remained on good terms following their split, and often speak fondly of their time together.

It became increasingly clear that Ariana's path was shifting toward the music industry, which placed mounting pressure on her commitments at Nickelodeon. As her frustrations with the role of Cat grew, so did the on-set tension between her and co-star Jennette McCurdy...

Ariana Grande performs as the opening act for Justin Bieber's Believe Tour in Atlanta on Saturday, August 10, 2013

Drama Queens

When *Sam & Cat* first aired in 2013, fans were excited to see Ariana Grande and Jennette McCurdy bring their beloved characters from *Victorious* and *iCarly* together in a fun-filled new series. However, as Ariana's music career took off, Jennette became increasingly vocal about her frustrations with the direction of the show, especially how her character, Sam, was being handled. Her dissatisfaction wasn't limited to the writing—it extended to the production environment as well. Having recently released her debut album, Ariana was often absent from set, leaving Jennette to "hold down the fort" while Ariana focused on her music career, attending award shows, recording new songs, and doing press.

In her 2022 bestselling memoir *I'm Glad My Mom Died*, Jennette openly described the anger she felt as she watched Ariana miss days of filming. The tipping point came when she was told

LEFT: Jennette McCurdy and Ariana Grande back in 2011 mock fighting

that Ariana would be absent for an entire week, and her absence would be written into the episode by having her character locked in a box. Jennette recalled the moment with frustration, saying, "So I have to turn down movies while Ariana's off whistle-toning at the Billboard Music Awards? F*ck. This."

As Ariana continued to rise in the music industry, Jennette began to feel sidelined. She couldn't help but compare her own career to Ariana's, who was landing magazine covers, performing at prestigious award shows, and appearing on "30 Under 30" lists. Meanwhile, Jennette was promoting lesser-known projects, including her work as the face of a tween clothing line.

The final straw for Jennette came when Ariana casually revealed she had spent the previous evening playing charades at the house of Tom Hanks, one of Hollywood's most beloved and legendary actors. Hearing this broke something inside Jennette. "That was the moment I broke," she said. "I couldn't take it anymore." The idea of Ariana, who was already excelling in music and TV, spending time with a national treasure like Tom Hanks was too much for Jennette to bear. "Pop star success I could handle, but hanging out with Sheriff Woody, with Forrest f*cking Gump? This has gone too far," she wrote in her memoir.

From that moment on, Jennette admitted she could no longer maintain a cordial relationship with Ariana. Every time Ariana missed work for another performance or event, Jennette saw it as a personal affront. The tension on set escalated further when Jennette became embroiled in a photo scandal during the filming of *Sam & Cat*. A series of private, suggestive photos of the 21-year-old actress were leaked online without her consent, sparking significant media attention and public scrutiny.

Ultimately, both Ariana Grande and Jennette McCurdy had outgrown their Nickelodeon roles, each pursuing different paths in their careers—Ariana focusing on her rapidly growing music career and Jennette yearning for more creative freedom and opportunities outside of television. This shift in their professional lives, compounded by the mounting tensions on set, led to the inevitable cancellation of *Sam & Cat* after just one season. While the show was successful in its own right, the evolving aspirations of its stars, coupled with behind-the-scenes struggles, made it clear that their time in the world of Nickelodeon was coming to an end, marking a turning point in their respective careers.

The "Challenging Second Album"

After a successful debut, artists are often thrust into the unforgiving spotlight of heightened expectations, with fans, critics, and industry executives eagerly waiting to see whether they can replicate, or even surpass, their initial success. A strong debut may introduce an artist as a promising new voice, but it's the second album that often determines whether they have true staying power. The so-called "challenging second album" may sound like a music industry cliché, but it's a myth grounded in hard truth. It reflects the very real pressure artists face to evolve creatively without alienating the fans who embraced them initially–creating a high-stakes balancing act that can define or derail a career. For Ariana Grande, this challenge was no exception.

Following the critical and commercial triumph of *Yours Truly*, expectations for her sophomore record were nothing short of enormous. The stakes were only amplified by Ariana's unique position in the entertainment world as a former child star attempting to redefine herself as a serious musical act, a shift that many performers struggle to manage without backlash. *Yours Truly* had introduced her as a fresh-faced newcomer with powerhouse vocals and a charming retro-R&B sound, but her next move would determine whether she could transcend her teen-star roots and fully step into the pop mainstream.

Ariana's highly anticipated second album, *My Everything*, was released on August 22, 2014. For the project, Ariana collaborated with an impressive roster of hitmakers and producers, including Max Martin, Shellback, Benny Blanco, Zedd, and David Guetta–a clear signal of her ambition to take her sound to the next level. Aiming to create what she described as an "evolution" from her debut, Ariana pushed into more mature and diverse musical territory. While still rooted in pop and R&B, the album expanded beyond the retro '90s influences of her first record and embraced a broader sonic palette, dabbling in EDM, electropop, and dance-pop. The album also featured an array of high-profile collaborations, with guest appearances from Iggy Azalea, Zedd, Big Sean, Cashmere Cat, Childish Gambino, The Weeknd, and A$AP Ferg, as well as Jessie J and Nicki Minaj on the deluxe edition. The result was a genre-blending, hit-packed release that firmly established Ariana as one of pop's most versatile and exciting voices.

ABOVE: Ariana performs to promote her album *My Everything* in Tokyo, Sept, 2014

TOP LEFT: *My Everything* album cover

Stellar Singles

Problem feat. Iggy Azalea

As the lead single, "Problem" shows Ariana shedding her sweet, girl-next-door image in favour of a bold, flirtatious and confident persona. The song combines bold saxophone riffs, whispery hooks, and explosive choruses, creating a dynamic and addictive pop experience. Lyrically, the song explores the emotional push and pull of a toxic relationship, with Ariana declaring she has "one less problem without you", capturing a blend of post-breakup empowerment and lingering vulnerability. The track includes some noteworthy features including Big Sean's work as an uncredited background vocalist where he delivers the iconic whispered vocals of the hook, as well as a slick verse from female Australian rapper Iggy Azalea.

In an interview with *MTV*, Ariana detailed her first meeting with the Aussie, saying "the first time I met Iggy we were at the EMAs actually in Amsterdam and we sort of bonded at the after party that night and I thought she was the coolest", "I fell in love with Iggy when I saw this video of her performing 'Work' live, and I just thought she was so original and I loved the way she pronounced her words... I thought we would make the perfect girl-power duo for 'Problem', so I'm very grateful that she did it with me".

"Problem" was an immediate commercial success, debuting at number three on the Billboard Hot 100 list, with 438,000 copies sold in its first week. The song later peaked at number two, becoming Ariana's highest-charting single. Internationally, "Problem" reached the coveted number one spot as it dominated the charts in Ireland, New Zealand and the United Kingdom.

The song's theme of liberation from a toxic relationship set the tone for the album's more mature direction. While discussing her album, the popstar said, "I wanted to experiment a bit more with this album and try some new sounds and things that weren't in my comfort zone because I feel like that's where some of the greatest work can come from, really pushing yourself to try something new".

Even the music video for the song further emphasized Ariana's transformation. With bold black-and-white visuals, mod-inspired fashion, and high-energy choreography, the video oozes confidence and style. Ariana sports thigh-high boots, high ponytails, and retro silhouettes—an aesthetic that would become central to her brand moving forward. The video's sharp, stylised visuals helped cement her new image.

Despite "Problem" becoming one of the most iconic songs released in 2014, Ariana initially "fell out of love" with the single and didn't want it featured on her second album. However, during an album listening session with her record label, "Problem" came on and the popstar instantly said "What the hell is wrong with me? Holy shit!", and promptly added it back onto the record.

My Everything was a runaway hit right from the get-go, debuting at number one on the *Billboard* 200 and selling over 169,000 copies in its first week. This achievement marked Ariana's second consecutive album to debut at the top of the charts, making her the first female artist since Susan Boyle to have both of her first two albums land the coveted number one spot in the United States. Ariana proved that she wasn't just a one-record wonder, but a rising star with immense staying power. *My Everything* was not only a sonic step forward for the young pop sensation, but it also marked a transition from the sweet, almost fairytale-like image Ariana had established on her debut, into a young woman with a more mature approach to love, life and sex. The marketing of *My Everything* was equally reflective of this change of direction. Gone were the days of pastel tones and playful innocence; in their place was a more sophisticated, and at times, "scandalizing" aesthetic. The album cover itself caused a stir, as it featured Ariana perched on a stool in a provocative pose, dressed in black lingerie and thigh-high boots—an image that sparked debate but undeniably positioned her as an adult artist in control of her brand. In interviews, Ariana addressed the shift, telling *Billboard* in 2014, "I've spent my life being this perfect goody-two-shoes, and I'm kind of over that now. I want to be able to express myself in a way that is genuine and honest".

ABOVE: Ariana Grande live on stage during her Honeymoon Tour in Fort Lauderdale, Florida, in 2015

LEFT: Iggy Azalea

Ariana performs her Honeymoon tour in Florida, 2015

All The Way to The White House

In the same year she released *My Everything*, Ariana reached another major milestone by performing at the White House. In March 2014, the young popstar was invited to take part in the prestigious "Women of Soul" concert, hosted by First Lady Michelle Obama. Other performers included Aretha Franklin, Patti LaBelle, Melissa Etheridge, Janelle Monáe, Tessanne Chin and Jill Scott. Ariana performed Whitney Houston's powerful ballad "I Have Nothing", as well as her own retro-inspired track "Tattooed Heart".

Just a month later, Ariana returned to the White House to perform at the annual Easter Egg Roll, entertaining a crowd of over 30,000 with a confident and playful rendition of "Right There". Dressed in an oversized lavender sweater and white go-go boots, she charmed both the crowd and the cameras. But for Ariana, the day's highlight wasn't the stage, but the meeting with her childhood hero, Jim Carrey, a moment she later described on Twitter as surreal and emotional: "Met my childhood crush Jim Carrey ... he was kind, warm and human. I'm so happy."

To be invited to perform not once, but twice, at the White House in such a short span of time is an extraordinary achievement for anyone, especially for a 21-year-old. It was a moment of national recognition that marked just how far she had come... However, Ariana would soon discover that the media could build someone up and just as quickly tear them down.

MAIN IMAGE: Nicki Minaj joins Ariana Grande onstage at the 2014 iHeartRadio Music Festival in Las Vegas on September 19, lighting up the MGM Grand Garden Arena

PHI

Jessie J and Ariana Grande perform at Q102's Jingle Ball in Philadelphia, 2014

Music, Romance and Headlines

Big Sean

Ariana began dating rapper Big Sean in 2014, marking one of her first high-profile relationships in the public eye. The pair first raised eyebrows with their flirty collab on the young popstar's track "Right There," and by the time they teamed up again for the sultry ballad "Best Mistake" off her second studio album, it was clear the sparks weren't just in the studio. The couple seemingly confirmed their relationship when they walked the 2015 Grammy red carpet together. Ariana and Big Sean's musical-turned-real-life chemistry had fans and tabloids buzzing and was widely covered by the media, with both stars gushing about each other in interviews and social media posts. While their relationship seemed strong, it came to an end in April 2015 after eight months of dating. Though the split was reportedly amicable, it marked the beginning of a recurring theme in Ariana's life: navigating love and heartbreak under the watchful gaze of the world.

Up until then, Ariana had received mostly positive press in the early stages of her career. Occasionally, there would be a few unfavourable reports or reviews published, but broadly speaking, much of the coverage about her was nice. However, there was a noticeable shift in 2014, when rumours of Ariana's diva-like behaviour began to surface. There

were whispers about abrupt interview walkouts, bodyguard-issued instructions to journalists, and reports that she had stormed out of photoshoots when things didn't go her way. Headlines like "Ariana Grande's Diva Demands Revealed!" became commonplace on the covers of gossip magazines. "I stopped doing interviews for a really long time because I felt like whenever I would get into a position where somebody would try to say something for clickbait or twist my words or blah, blah, blah, I would defend myself", Ariana explained in an interview with Zane Lowe for Apple Music, "And then, people would be like, 'Oh, she's a diva.' I was like, 'This doesn't make any sense'". The term "diva" is loaded one, especially when applied to women in the entertainment industry. Where male artists might be described as "assertive" or "in control," women are often labelled "difficult" or "divas" for exhibiting the same behaviour. Former collaborator Jessie J, was quick to come to Ariana's defence and addressed this double standard head-on, saying, "I always say, judge a person when you meet them...I've met Ariana, and there's a very thin line between 'diva' and 'survival'" adding, "I've had the diva stuff. And it's when people can't cope with how passionate you are, and how much you care". For Ariana, setting boundaries, whether in interviews, performances, or public appearances, was not about being demanding, but about protecting her peace, her image, and her work.

ABOVE: Big Sean and Ariana Grande perform together during KIIS-FM's Jingle Ball in Los Angeles, 2014

The Diva Diaries (A Timeline)

Australian Photoshoot

While promoting her album *My Everything* in Australia, Ariana agreed to a photo shoot and interview with several members of the Australian media. However, things reportedly went south when she allegedly became unhappy with the lighting, angles, and the overall creative direction of the shoot. According to press reports, Ariana abruptly walked out after just a few photos were taken, reportedly asking that the images already shot be deleted. Sources claimed she had a strict list of conditions which included being photographed only from her left side and her refusal to be shot in natural light. She also apparently banned the following topics from the interview questions as she deemed them "too personal":

(1) Relationships/Dating/Ex-boyfriends

(2) Mariah Carey

(3) *Sam & Cat*/Jennette McCurdy

(4) Working/collaborating with Justin Bieber

(5) Her grandfather passing away

The walkout caused a media frenzy in Australia, with several journalists speaking out and accusing the star of being "difficult" and "controlling." One photographer told *The Daily Telegraph* that she had stormed out without explanation, while others accused her team of heavily micromanaging the shoot and interview process. Ariana's camp later dismissed many of the claims as exaggerated, with sources close to her insisting she was simply standing up for how she wanted to be presented, especially in a media landscape that can be unforgiving to young female celebrities. Still, the damage was done.

Awkward Fan Encounters

While visiting a New York radio station in the summer of 2014, the 21-year-old pop star came under fire when an industry insider shared an astonishing story about Ariana with the *New York Daily News*, saying, "She did autographs and pics and was all smiles until she got into the elevator, and as soon as the doors shut she said, ' hope they all f***ing die'". After the incident, more and more people took to social media to post about their own unfortunate encounters with the singer. One father of a self-professed "Arianator" documented his experience meeting Ariana in a blog post, writing "Jen and the other MTV winner (a young man of 16 who travelled across the entire country for this meeting) were interviewed on camera by MTV to be broadcast at a later date. Before the camera rolled, they were told they would be asked what it was like meeting Ariana, and they had to PRETEND that they had already had said meeting, even though the interview was taped BEFORE Ariana ever appeared. They were told what to say, almost word for word. I know Jen feared that if she refused to do this, she would not meet Ariana (though she was not told that)". He went on to say that the actual meet up with the popstar wasn't much better, "Ms. Grande glanced at the photo on Jen's phone and said, 'Let's redo that picture', she said nothing else, so Jen retook the photo. No peace sign from Ari this time. Then, Jen took out one of the drawings that won the contest for her. Kelly snapped a photo of her smiling little sister giving Ariana the drawing. 'Delete those pictures, please', was all Ariana said. 'Can I just keep the one of my sister showing you the drawing?' asked Kel". Ariana apparently turned to her security and ordered, "Make sure she deleted those".

#DoughnutGate

In July 2015, security footage leaked of Ariana inside a Californian donut shop with one of her backup dancers, where the popstar can be seen licking several donuts on display without purchasing them before jumping up and down, laughing. Then, when an employee approached the pair with a tray full of doughnuts, the singer turned to her male companion and loudly professed, "What the f*** is that? I hate Americans. I hate America". The clip went viral almost instantly, igniting a wave of backlash and outrage across social media, morning shows, and news outlets. Critics slammed Ariana for being disrespectful, unhygienic, and unpatriotic, while headlines branded her a spoiled star spiralling out of control.

Ariana quickly issued a public apology in the form of a YouTube video, stating 'I am EXTREMELY proud to be an American, and I've always made it clear that I love my country.' Ariana added: "What I said in a private moment with my friend, who was buying the donuts, was taken out of context, and I am sorry for not using more discretion with my choice of words". She continued, by saying, "As an advocate for healthy eating, food is very important to me and I sometimes get upset by how freely we as Americans eat and consume things without giving any thought to the consequences that it has on our health and society as a whole". "Seeing a video of yourself behaving poorly, that you have no idea was taken, is such a rude awakening, that you don't know what to do – I was so disgusted with myself" "Not here to make any excuses or justify my behaviour, because I can't. ... I'm just here to apologize". While some fans brushed it off as a youthful lapse in judgment, others saw it as further proof that fame was going to Ariana's head. The now infamous #DoughnutGate debacle, though seemingly harmless, did have professional repercussions for the singer as the Democratic National Committee (DNC) staffers were rumoured to have cancelled her performance at a White House event later that year. Despite this setback, Ariana didn't let the negative press get her down. She was determined to come back stronger than ever.

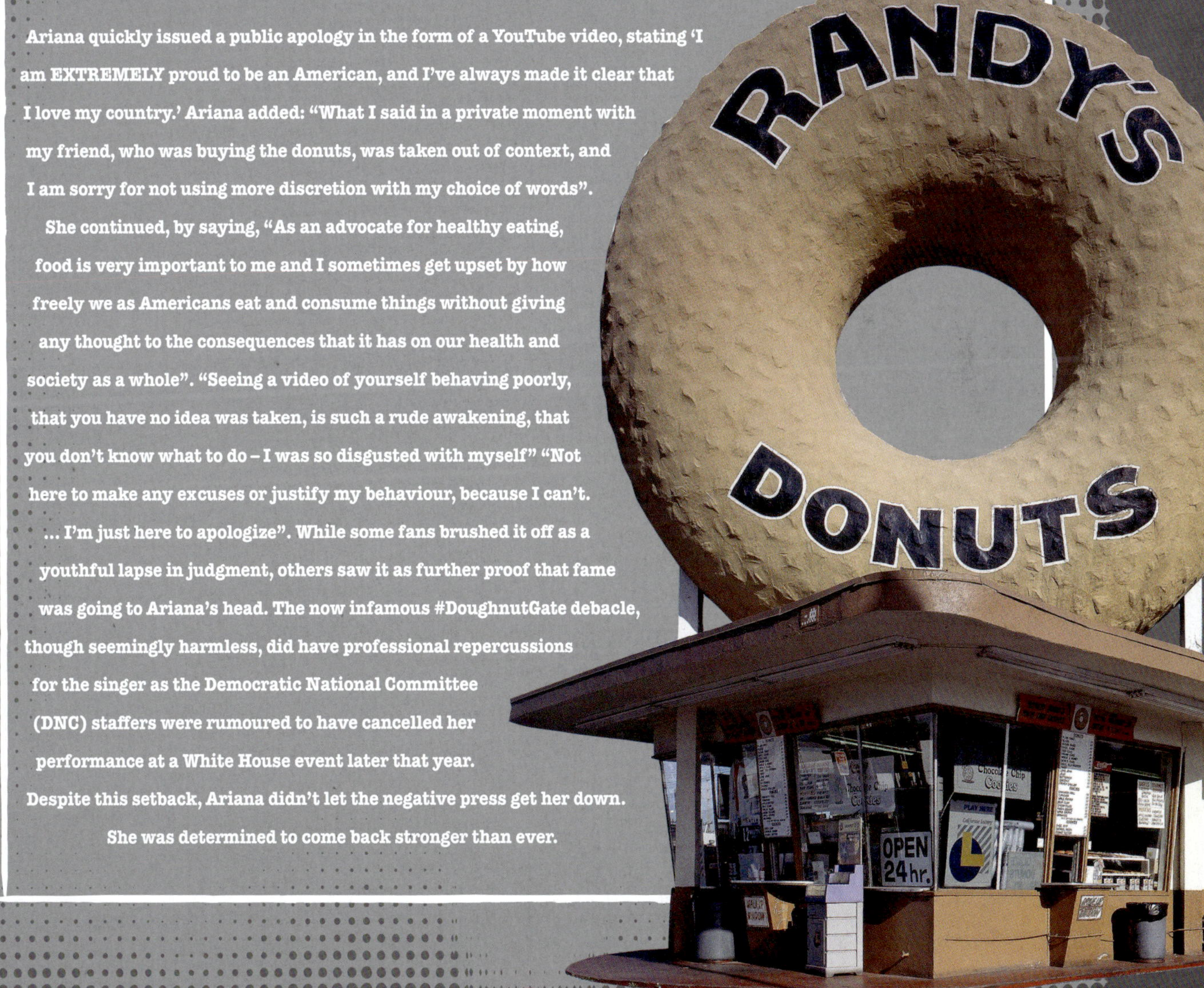

Let The Music Speak

In the wake of mounting controversies, Ariana found herself at a crossroads. The headlines were becoming louder than the music, and for a moment, it seemed her career might veer off course. But instead of spiralling or lashing out at critics, Ariana did something far more powerful: she went quiet, and she got to work. While the media continued to dissect her every move, Ariana was back in the studio, fine-tuning her sound and shaping the next phase of her artistry. Just over a year after the release of her sophomore album *My Everything*, the pop sensation came back bigger than ever with her brand new single *"Focus"*.

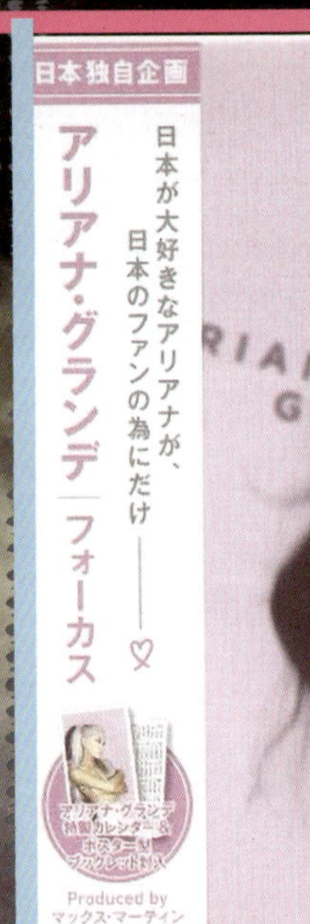

MAIN IMAGE: Ariana Grande at the 2016 MTV Movie Awards held at Warner Bros. Studios in California, 2016

LEFT: Japanese cover edition of Ariana's single Focus

2015-2016

Stellar Singles

Focus

Released on October 30, 2015, "Focus" marked Ariana's glittering return to the pop spotlight. This bold, brassy anthem was aimed squarely at her haters but also served as a way for Ariana to regain control of her narrative amid growing media scrutiny.

Ariana announced the single during her September 2015 appearance on *The Tonight Show Starring Jimmy Fallon*, revealing that it would drop later that October. In the lead-up to its release, she stirred excitement across social media with cryptic teases, posting lyric snippets, audio and video previews, and even pixelated versions of the single's cover art. On October 14, the official artwork was finally revealed, showcasing Ariana bathed in cool, celestial tones, sporting icy platinum blonde hair, a striking departure from her usual look. Dressed in a minimal, futuristic outfit and seated in a spotlight against a stark lavender background, the image signalled yet another bold reinvention. A week before the single dropped, a 15-second teaser of "Focus" made its debut in a commercial for Ari by Ariana Grande, her first fragrance, perfectly blending music promotion with her growing brand empire.

The song's funky, horn-laced chorus, featuring the booming voice of Jamie Foxx repeating the now-iconic phrase 'Focus on me', might, at first glance, seem self-centred. But Ariana flipped that narrative. "When I say, "Focus on me", I'm not asking to be the centre of attention. I'm not asking you to focus on my face or my clothes or my body or my singing voice" explained the popstar, "By 'focus on me', I literally mean focus on me. Focus on what I'm all about and what I believe in. The more we focus on each other as people and not on what we look like, what we're wearing, our gender, our hairstyle, our sexuality, the colour of our skin. But focus on each other on a soul level. The more we realize how much we have in common, the more we listen to each other, the more one we become".

The music video for "Focus", directed by Hannah Lux Davis fully leaned into Ariana's evolving aesthetic. The video quickly racked up millions of views and, for several years, remained one of her most watched. Even though "Focus" didn't end up on the main album, it served its purpose—sending a clear message: Ariana Grande wasn't letting the noise distract her. She was focused, empowered, and letting her music do the talking.

Despite the song's strong message and catchy lyrics, "Focus" received mixed reviews from fans and music critics alike. Listeners were quick to praise Ariana's powerhouse vocals and the song's brassy production, but criticized its similarity to her 2014 hit "Problem". Ariana's return onto the music scene wasn't as explosive as she might've hoped for, but instead of giving up, she took this experience and used it to come back even stronger.

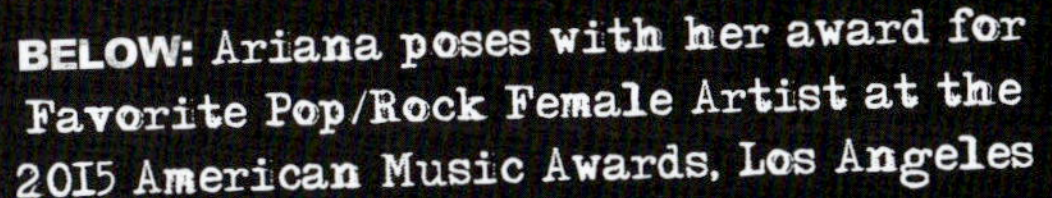
BELOW: Ariana poses with her award for Favorite Pop/Rock Female Artist at the 2015 American Music Awards, Los Angeles

BOTTOM LEFT: Jamie Foxx

By 2016, Ariana was done playing it safe. After two successful albums and a string of chart-topping singles, she was ready to rewrite the rules of her own narrative. With her third studio album entitled *Dangerous Woman*, she shed the last remnants of her Nickelodeon persona and leaned fully into an era of bold artistic identity, sensual empowerment, and genre experimentation. The title said it all. This was no longer the sweet girl next door. This was a woman stepping fully into her power. At the centre of this reinvention was the iconic album cover, featuring Ariana in a sleek, strapless black outfit, her signature high ponytail perfectly in place, and a glossy black latex bunny mask perched over her eyes. The mask, equal parts playful and provocative, became the defining symbol of the era, suggesting themes of mystery, strength, and sensuality. Gone were the bubble-gum hues of her earlier visuals and in their place stood a more grown-up aesthetic with high fashion looks, monochrome palettes, and confident poses.

While *Dangerous Woman* ultimately marked a powerful evolution for Ariana, the album went through several transformations, creative detours, and even a last-minute change of title before fully taking shape. The singer had begun working on her third album all the way back in October 2014, just two months after the release of *My Everything*. Initially titled *Moonlight*, Ariana envisioned the project as something more personal, romantic, and tender than her previous work. She even teased fans with cryptic crescent moon imagery across social media and revealed in interviews that one of the album's earliest tracks, also titled *Moonlight*, had been inspired by a "very cute night" with then-boyfriend Ricky Álvarez. Throughout 2015, between performances on her Honeymoon Tour, Ariana was hard at work in the music studio, recording and collaborating with longtime friends such as Tommy Brown and Victoria Monét. In the early stages, *Moonlight* seemed to be leaning into a softer, dreamy sound, a continuation of the romanticism and R&B flair she had explored on *My Everything*. However, by late 2015, things started to shift. The release of her lead single "Focus" received a lukewarm response. While the song debuted at No. 7 on the Billboard Hot 100 and was praised for Ariana's vocals, critics felt it tread too-familiar ground and described the Jamie Foxx feature as "grating." Though she initially called "Focus" a bridge between *My Everything* and *Moonlight*, the underwhelming reception prompted her to rethink the direction of the album entirely. "*Moonlight* is a lovely song, and it's a lovely title. It's really romantic, and it definitely ties together the old music and the new music, but *Dangerous Woman* is a lot stronger", commented the singer on the change of creative direction. Ariana announced in early 2016 that the project would instead be called *Dangerous Woman*, explaining to fans that the name better represented where she was personally and artistically. "To me, a dangerous woman is someone who's not afraid to take a stand, be herself, and to be honest," she told *Billboard*. And that spirit permeates the entire record.

Stellar Singles

Dangerous Woman

The title track and lead single off Ariana's third studio album, "Dangerous Woman", is a smoky, sultry power ballad that marked a definitive turning point in her artistic evolution. From the very first note, the song oozes confidence and seduction. Musically, "Dangerous Woman", with its moody guitar riffs, dark cinematic undercurrent, and brooding tempo, wouldn't feel out of place in a James Bond opening credits sequence. The production is also intentionally restrained, giving Ariana's vocals the space to simmer and soar. She moves effortlessly between

breathy vulnerability and powerhouse belting, crafting a vocal performance that's rich with emotion and command. Lyrically, the song captures the tension between surrender and control, between softness and power. Ariana isn't being possessed or overpowered by love; she's choosing to let her guard down, and in doing so, finding strength.

Many listeners and critics noted the Rihanna-esque energy running throughout the track, particularly the smouldering, unapologetic sensual vibe Rihanna is known for. This isn't a coincidence: "Dangerous Woman" was originally written with Carrie Underwood in mind, but as the song became more scandalous in nature, it was then pitched to both Rihanna and Alicia Keys before Ariana eventually picked it up.

ABOVE: Cover of Ariana Grande's third album, *Dangerous Woman*

Into You

"Into You" stands as one of the most defining tracks of Ariana's entire discography. It is a masterfully crafted dance-pop anthem that merges seductive atmosphere with high-voltage energy, a shining example that the popstar was now fully in command of her own sound.

Produced by pop heavyweights Max Martin and Ilya Salmanzadeh, the song opens with a minimal, moody beat before building into an explosive chorus layered with shimmering synths and pulsating rhythms. The structure is impeccably designed to create tension: it starts slow, almost teasing, and then swells into a massive, euphoric release that feels tailor-made for the dancefloor.

What makes "Into You" such an enduring success though, is its uncanny ability to feel grandiose, almost cinematic in scope, yet deeply personal all at once. Critics and fans alike praised the track for its sonic maturity and intensely sleek and modern production.

Side to Side (Feat. Nicki Minaj)

By far the most talked about (and cheekiest) track from the *Dangerous Woman* era, "Side to Side" is a bona fide reggae-pop banger. The song opens with a laid-back, tropical beat, immediately setting it apart from the rest of the album's more sultry and dramatic offerings. The breezy island rhythms combined with bold lyrics loaded with double entendres, makes *"Side to Side"* the perfect summer bop. The track also marked one of Ariana's most memorable collaborations, this time with rap queen Nicki Minaj, whose razor-sharp verse brought edge and attitude to the song. The duo's chemistry was effortless, blending Ariana's sultry vocals with Nicki's commanding energy to create a pop-rap hybrid that dominated charts.

The music video for *"Side to Side"* was equally as iconic as it further leaned into the song's tongue-in-cheek tone. Set in a neon-lit gym, Ariana is seen dressed in pastel workout gear leading a spin class to amplify the song's themes of physical exhaustion and romantic escapade. This is all expressed through hilariously on-the-nose choreography that would be considered more seductive than sweaty. The result is a visual and sonic statement that's campy, confident, and entirely self-aware.

MAIN IMAGE: Ariana putting on a performance at the grand opening of T-Mobile Arena in Las Vegas, April, 2016

LEFT: Nicki Minaj

Commercially, *Dangerous Woman* earned 175,000 units in its first week and landed at number two on the US Billboard 200, blocked from the top spot by Drake's latest album *Views*. While it was her only studio album not to debut at number one, *Dangerous Woman* has since become one of her most beloved and enduring records among fans. Its mature themes, bold sonic shifts, and empowered visuals helped solidify Ariana's transformation into a full-fledged pop powerhouse, proving that chart position isn't always the best measure of long-term impact.

Grace Under Fire

Coming off the heels of her most ambitious and transformative era to date, *Dangerous Woman* officially cemented Ariana's place in pop royalty. The singer well and truly proved that she wasn't just another fleeting moment in pop culture, but rather a bona fide musical force with staying power, vision, and undeniable influence. Now, with the weight of proving herself behind her, Ariana began to focus her energy on exploring the full range of her creative and personal pursuits, starting off with a brief return to the small screen.

In December 2016, Ariana returned to her theatrical roots with a starring role in NBC's *Hairspray Live!*, the networks fourth entry in its series of made-for-TV musical telecasts, behind *The Wiz Live!*, *Peter Pan Live!*, and *The Sound of Music Live!*. Cast as Penny Pingleton, the sweet and slightly awkward best friend to Tracy Turnblad, played by Maddie Baillio, Ariana's performance was both charming and vocally impressive. But most importantly it was an opportunity for the pop star to show off yet another facet of her artistry.

MAIN IMAGE: Ariana Grande arrives at the *Hairspray Live!* press junket in California, 2016

2016-2017

The Plot

Set in 1960s Baltimore, *Hairspray* follows the story of Tracy Turnblad (Maddie Baillio), a big-hearted and big-haired teenager who dreams of dancing on her favourite TV program, *The Corny Collins Show.* But when Tracy wins a spot on the program against all odds, she soon uses her newfound fame to challenge the show's racially segregated format and promote inclusivity. Alongside her quirky best friend Penny Pingleton (Ariana Grande), the suave Seaweed J. Stubbs (Ephraim Sykes), and his mother Motormouth Maybelle (Jennifer Hudson), a bold, no-nonsense advocate for racial integration, Tracy spearheads a campaign to make the show inclusive, whist also navigating her crush on resident dream boat Link Larkin (Garrett Clayton). Meanwhile, her loving but anxious mother Edna (Harvey Fierstein) and eccentric father Wilbur (Martin Short) offer comic relief and emotional grounding, reminding audiences that change starts at home. Antagonists like the snobbish Velma Von Tussle (Kristin Chenoweth) and her daughter Amber (Dove Cameron) add tension and reinforce the societal pressures Tracy must overcome. Bursting with catchy tunes, humour, and heart, *Hairspray* is a joyful but pointed celebration of self-love, equality, and social justice. While many viewers were familiar with the star-studded 2007 film adaptation, starring Nikki Blonsky and John Travolta, NBC's *Hairspray Live!* offered a fresh and exhilarating take on the beloved musical. With its dynamic cast, fast-paced scene transitions, and the thrill of real-time performance, the live broadcast captured both the nostalgia and urgency of the original, offering a theatrical experience right in the comfort of the viewer's living room.

RIGHT: Ariana Grande as Penny Pingleton

The show was a huge hit for NBC, far outperforming any of the network's previous live musicals. On Rotten Tomatoes, the special holds a 76% rating with the site's consensus stating, "*Hairspray Live!* shimmers with outstanding performances, an engaging story, and songs that let its stars shine". Ariana's performance was particularly well reviewed, with many critics praising her comedic timing. Sonia Saraiya of the magazine *Variety* wrote that it "took a few musical numbers to settle into a rhythm. But once it did the musical easily became the best NBC has attempted. [...] Ariana Grande, certifiable pop star, came away as the show's MVP, acting as both reliably overlook-able sidekick and, once the situation required it, showstopping diva". *Hairspray Live!* served as a refreshing reminder to fans—and to Ariana herself—of her humble beginnings in the world of musical theatre. The singer came away from the experience with an immense amount of gratitude, saying "It's so great to be part of something so special. I grew up loving Hairspray, so to perform in it live on national television felt like a dream come true", in a behind-the-scenes interview.

As Ariana hit new heights on stage, her personal life was meanwhile quietly blossoming with a new romance.

Music, Romance and Headlines

Mac Miller

Before their relationship turned romantic, Ariana and Mac Miller (born Malcolm James McCormick) were friends for a long time. The two first met in 2012 when Ariana was just 19, after a flirty Twitter exchange led them to collaborate on a remake of the 1944 Christmas hit, "Baby It's Cold Outside". Despite the pair's undeniable chemistry on the track, the sparks apparently never left the studio.

Their friendship and musical collaboration reached a wider audience in March 2013 with the release of Ariana's single, "The Way" which featured a guest verse from the Pittsburgh native rapper. The accompanying music video was packed with PDA and even ended with a surprise kiss between the two artists, only fuelling rumours that the pair were more than friends. Ariana was quick to shut down any speculation, insisting the kiss was just part of the video's direction and that she and Mac were strictly friends, though that didn't stop fans from shipping the couple hard. Mac would even occasionally pop up at her live performances of "The Way" throughout 2013. Though the pair would wait years before collaborating publicly again, Ariana and Mac's friendship continued to grow behind the scenes until eventually something deeper blossomed in 2016. Just days after Ariana's backup dancer Ricky Álvarez, fans began spotting the singer spending time with Mac again, most notably on a trip to Disneyland with mutual friend Victoria Monét. The timing raised eyebrows, but the rumours were quickly confirmed when the two were seen kissing outside a sushi restaurant in late August. That same month, Mac jumped on a remix of Ariana's hit "Into You", adding yet a new track to the pair's musical legacy. Mac also featured Ariana on "My Favourite Part", a romantic standout from his 2016 album *The Divine Feminine*.

Ariana said of their relationship, "We weren't ready at all. We both needed to experience some things, but the love has been there the whole time." In 2017, the couple made more public appearances, attending Coachella together, sharing adorable moments on Instagram, and performing their hit "The Way" during a surprise duet on Ariana's Dangerous Woman Tour.

But beyond the cute posts and stage cameos was a deeply meaningful connection that Ariana would later describe as both beautiful and complicated. Their relationship was full of love, laughter, and creativity, but also marked by Mac's ongoing struggles with addiction—something Ariana would speak about with candour and compassion after their eventual breakup.

TOP RIGHT: Ariana and Mac Miller at the Cincinnati Bengals vs. Pittsburgh Steelers game at Heinz Field in Pittsburgh, 2016

Beauty And the Beat

In 2017, Ariana Grande added her voice to one of Disney's most beloved fairytales, contributing to the live-action remake of *Beauty and the Beast*. Teaming up with Grammy-winning singer John Legend, the pair recorded a powerful rendition of the film's iconic title track, originally sung by Angela Lansbury in the 1991 animated classic. The accompanying music video, directed by Dave Meyers, placed Ariana in an opulent red gown as she performed in a grand ballroom, effectively mirroring the iconic dance scene between Belle and the Beast. The collaboration not only introduced her to a new generation of Disney fans but also demonstrated her versatility as a vocalist. For Ariana, the project was more than just another feature but another full-circle moment, tying back to her childhood love of Disney and musical theatre. The single was nominated for a Teen Choice Award and received praise for its emotional gravitas, making it a standout in both the film's soundtrack and Ariana's ever-growing list of memorable collaborations.

With a hit Disney duet under her belt, a blossoming romance with Mac Miller, and her theatrical roots shining once again, Ariana was soaring higher than ever. The popstar showed no sign of slowing down, and instead prepared to take centre stage again to embark on the Dangerous Woman Tour. Kicking off in Phoenix, Arizona in February 2017, the tour promised to be a global celebration of her artistic evolution. Spanning more than 75 dates across North America, Europe, Asia, and Latin America, the show was a masterclass in pop spectacle. Each night, Ariana captivated crowds with hypnotic choreography, cinematic visuals, and flawless vocals that reminded everyone why she was one of her generation's most gifted performers. With all the excitement surrounding her upcoming world tour, no one could have anticipated how drastically and tragically it would come to redefine the young popstar's life.

RIGHT: Poster for Dangerous Woman World Tour 2017

DANGEROUS WOMAN TOUR
ARIANA GRANDE

On stage during the Dangerous Woman Tour opener at Talking Stick Resort Arena, Phoenix, Arizona on February 3, 2017

Ariana reaching out to the audience during the opening night of her Dangerous Woman Tour in Phoenix, Arizona, February 3, 2017

I ♥ MANCHESTER
POLAND LOVE YOU

On May 22, 2017, what should have been another triumphant night on the Dangerous Woman Tour turned into one of the darkest moments in recent music history. As thousands of fans, many of them children and teens, were exiting the Manchester Arena, a suicide bomber detonated an explosive device in the foyer, killing 22 people and injuring hundreds more. Ariana had just finished performing and was backstage when the explosion occurred. Her mother, Joan Grande, who had been in the front row, reportedly helped escort frightened fans backstage and stayed with them until they could be taken to safety. The attack, one of the deadliest in the recent UK memory, shocked the world and devastated the singer. In the early hours of the next morning, Ariana tweeted simply: "broken. from the bottom of my heart, I am so so sorry. I don't have words". The singer immediately flew back to her hometown of Boca Raton to be with her family and Mac before staying silent for several days to process everything. On May 26, Ariana announced that she would host a benefit concert in Manchester for the victims of the attack, proving that even in the face of unspeakable horror, the 23-year-old found a way to respond with empathy, love, and unity.

LEFT: Floral tribute honoring the 22 victims of the terror attack at Ariana Grande's Manchester Arena concert

ABOVE: Ariana with The Black Eyed Peas during the One Love Manchester benefit concert at Old Trafford Cricket Ground, June 4, 2017

One Love Manchester

On June 4, 2017, less than two weeks after the tragedy, Ariana organized and headlined the One Love Manchester concert at Old Trafford Cricket Ground. The event, attended by 55,000 people, featured performances by renowned artists including Justin Bieber, the Black Eyed Peas, Coldplay, Miley Cyrus, Mac Miller, Marcus Mumford, Niall Horan, Little Mix, Katy Perry, Take That, Imogen Heap, Victoria Monét, Pharrell Williams, Robbie Williams, U2 and Liam Gallagher. The concert was broadcast live across multiple platforms and reached audiences in over 50 countries. It raised more than £10 million within 12 hours, contributing to the We Love Manchester Emergency Fund established to aid victims and their families.

The concert was marked by many powerful and beautiful moments, but one song in particular took on a life of its own. Originally released in 2014 as a single from Ariana's album *My Everything*, the track had long been a fan favourite. However, in the aftermath of the Manchester attack, its lyrics, centred around one final moment with a loved one, took on a heartbreaking new meaning. The song "One Last Time" became an unofficial anthem for the victims and all those affected by the tragedy. During the One Love Manchester concert, Ariana led the audience in a tear-filled performance of her 2014 track, with 55,000 voices singing along in unison, with many of the people in the crowd holding photos of the victims.

In the weeks that followed, "One Last Time" surged up the charts again, this time not as a pop hit, but as a symbol of hope and unity. For Ariana, it became one of the most emotional and meaningful performances of her career.

MAIN IMAGE: Ariana on stage during the One Love Manchester benefit concert at Old Trafford Cricket Ground in England on June 4, 2017.

A Sweeter Sound

By the start of 2018, Ariana's life was once again shifting, only this time, it wasn't on stage or in the studio. It was in her personal life, where love, heartbreak, grief, and healing would all come crashing down in rapid succession.

Ariana's nearly two-year relationship with rapper Mac Miller had run its course and by May of that year the singer shared a note on social media confirming their split: "I respect and adore him endlessly and am grateful to have him in my life in any form, at all times regardless of how our relationship changes or what the universe holds for each of us!". Though the split was described as amicable, it was clear that it came with emotional weight. The two had supported each other through music, public appearances, and private milestones, but Ariana had made it clear that the relationship had reached an unhealthy point. Less than two weeks following the couple's breakup, Mac Miller made headlines when he was arrested for a hit-and-run after driving drunk. The rapper's struggle with addiction had been well documented through the years, but many of his fans were quick to point the finger at Arianaa for his sudden downfall. "I am not a babysitter or a mother and no woman should feel that they need to be", said the singer, as she clapped back to those who blamed her for Mac's struggles with addiction, "I have cared for him and tried to support his sobriety and prayed for his balance for years (and always will of course) but shaming/blaming women for a man's inability to keep it together is a very major problem". It was a rare moment of unfiltered honesty from the singer, but it offered fans a glimpse into her life caring for an addict.

Ariana didn't let her recent hardship drag her down, as less than a month after announcing her breakup, the singer was pictured on the cover of every magazine with *Saturday Night Live* cast member, Pete Davidson.

MAIN IMAGE: Ariana performing during the March for Our Lives rally in Washington, DC, on March 24, 2018, galvanized by a school shooting at a Florida high school

MAIN IMAGE: Ariana Grande performs during the 2018 Coachella Valley Music and Arts Festival in Indio, California, in April 2018

Stellar Singles

no tears left to cry

Released as the album's lead single in April 2018, "no tears left to cry" marked Ariana's triumphant return to music following the Manchester bombing. The song opens in a melancholic, dreamy tone before shifting into an upbeat bop that celebrates emotional resilience. Its genre-bending production and unexpected mood switch were reflective of her inner transformation as she shows the way grief had shaped her, but didn't define her. The accompanying music video, directed by Dave Meyers, showcased Ariana defying gravity as she walks across walls and ceilings, further amplifying her feelings of confusion. Critics praised the track for its bold, unexpected optimism, and it quickly became one of her signature hits, peaking at No. 3 on the Billboard Hot 100.

god is a woman

One of the most provocative and empowering tracks on *Sweetener,* "god is a woman" blends ethereal pop with trap beats and gospel harmonies to create an anthem of divine femininity. In the song, Ariana equates sensuality and confidence with spiritual power, delivering lines that assert female strength not just as equal to male authority, but as a cosmic force. The production is layered and dramatic, building to a climax that features a choral breakdown reminiscent of a church hymn. The stunning, surreal music video, also directed by Meyers, features Ariana literally painting the universe and floating in a cosmic womb, all while voicing female empowerment. The song debuted at No. 11 and eventually reached No. 8 on the Billboard Hot 100 but it also proved that Ariana wasn't just singing love songs anymore—she was making statements.

breathin

One of the most emotionally raw tracks on *Sweetener*, Ariana pulls back the curtain on her experience with anxiety and PTSD following the Manchester attack. The lyrics are simple, almost mantra-like, repeating the importance of just "keep breathin" during moments of panic and chaos. Produced by Ilya and Savan Kotecha, the track overlays Ariana's smooth vocals with ambient synths and pulsing rhythms, reflecting the sensation of trying to stay calm amid inner turbulence. The song became a fan-favourite, not just for its catchiness, but for its vulnerability and relatability.

Ariana Grande bringing the stage to life during the 2018 Billboard Music Awards in Las Vegas

Themes of confusion are obviously reflected throughout the music but also in the packaging of the record too. The album features a washed-out, upside-down portrait of the pop star, visually encapsulating the emotional disorientation she was experiencing during this tumultuous chapter of her life. "We've messed with the idea of not being able to find the ground again" she told *Time,* "Because I feel like I'm finally landing back on my feet now". Writing on social media, she gave an even richer explanation. She said that the inspiration for the upside-down theme was when she showed a friend sitting opposite her a picture, and "he said, 'I even love it upside-down' and that was kind of it for me. At the time I had been feeling very 'upside-down' for a while and the simplicity of that was like, 'oh duh, wow, my bestie a genius.'"

Ariana had done the impossible—she turned unimaginable pain into beauty, rising from tragedy to create something hopeful and healing. But just as she seemed to find her footing again, heartbreak came crashing back into her life with devastating force.

On September 7, 2018, less than six months after their breakup, Mac Miller tragically died from an accidental overdose at the age of 26. The news shook the music world but more importantly devastated Ariana. Though they were no longer together, Mac had remained a significant part of her life. Ariana went dark on social media for a few days, only reemerging to post a silent black-and-white video of Mac laughing, followed by a heartfelt caption. "I adored you from the day I met you when I was nineteen and I always will," she wrote. "I'm so sorry I couldn't fix or take your pain away. I really wanted to". The singer later revealed in an interview the intricacies of her relationship with Mac, saying "He was the best person ever, and he didn't deserve the demons he had. I was the glue for such a long time, and I found myself becoming... less and less sticky. The pieces just started to float away".

The aftermath of Mac's passing cast a heavy shadow over her engagement to Pete. As she mourned her ex-boyfriend, the cracks in her whirlwind romance deepened. Just over a month later, in October, Ariana and Pete called off their engagement. And though the breakup was sudden it was not surprising. In many ways, their relationship had been a coping mechanism built on escape rather than stability.

MAIN IMAGE: Mac Miller and Ariana Grande at an Oscar party together in Los Angeles, California, in 2018

Wicked Game

In October 2018, Ariana yet again showcased her ability to keep going—and keep performing—despite everything happening in her personal life. She returned to her musical theatre roots and talents, and performed "The Wizard and I" during NBC's *A Very Wicked Halloween*, a special celebrating the 15th anniversary of the Broadway musical *Wicked*. Dressed in a green ensemble with matching green lipstick, Ariana delivered a powerful rendition of Elphaba's signature song, demonstrating her vocal prowess. This performance was particularly poignant, marking her first major appearance following her split from Pete Davidson, but more importantly served as subtle foreshadowing for a major moment in her career still to come.

MAIN IMAGE: Ariana Grande performs live during NBC's A Very Wicked Halloween, celebrating 15 years of Wicked on Broadway in 2018

Stellar Singles

thank u, next

Written in the emotional aftermath of two of the most pivotal moments in her life, the song could have easily been a sombre ballad. Instead, Ariana flipped the script. "thank u, next" was light, reflective, and shockingly mature, offering gratitude for past relationships rather than bitterness or regret. Over a breezy, mid-tempo pop-R&B beat, Ariana name-checks four of her most public romances including Big Sean, Ricky Álvarez, Mac Miller, and Pete Davidson, giving each of the men a gracious nod. "thank u, next" quickly became more than just a hit single, it was a cultural touchstone, transforming into a catchphrase, a meme, and a mantra all at once. It debuted at No. 1 on the Billboard Hot 100, becoming Ariana's first chart-topping single in the U.S. and holding the top spot for seven non-consecutive weeks. It also shattered multiple streaming records, as it became the fastest song to reach 100 million streams on Spotify (in just 11 days) and held the record for most-streamed debut by a female artist on the platform at the time. The song would go on to be certified eight-times platinum in the U.S. and was named Apple Music's most-streamed song by a woman in 2019. But the true cultural moment came with the release of the song's music video. Directed by Hannah Lux Davis, the video was a nostalgic love letter to early-2000s teen movies, parodying *Mean Girls*, *Legally Blonde*, *13 Going on 30*, and *Bring It On*. Ariana seamlessly embodied each role, with cameos from close friends and even some original cast members from the films. The clip became an instant viral sensation, setting a YouTube record with over 55 million views in just 24 hours and reaching 100 million faster than any Vevo video at the time. But beyond the accolades and statistics, "thank u, next" captured the cultural zeitgeist with its empowering message: that healing, growth, and self-love can flourish in the aftermath of heartbreak. For Ariana, it was the ultimate act of reclaiming her narrative. For the world, it was a pop masterclass in turning pain into power.

MAIN IMAGE: Ariana posing for the cameras at the 13th Annual Women in Music event in New York City, December 2018

In the final weeks of 2018, just as "thank u, next" was reaching its cultural peak, Ariana gave fans an intimate look behind the scenes of one of the most defining periods of her life. On November 29, 2018, she released a four-part docuseries titled *Ariana Grande: Dangerous Woman Diaries* in collaboration with YouTube. Far from being a glossy promotional piece, the series was a vulnerable and cinematic reflection of Ariana's journey through fame, grief, growth, and resilience. The docuseries chronicled her whirlwind Dangerous Woman Tour, interweaving on-stage highlights with raw behind-the-scenes moments, including candid rehearsal footage, emotional glimpses of Ariana with her team, and touching tributes to the One Love Manchester benefit concert. Directed by long-time collaborator Alfredo Flores, the series blended glamour with authenticity, offering fans a deeper connection to Ariana not just as a pop star, but as a person still navigating her way through public tragedy and private healing.

On top of releasing a hit song and brand-new documentary series, Ariana had even more to smile about when she was named the Billboard Woman of the Year for 2018. The award was a recognition not just of her chart-topping hits or viral music videos, but of the strength

she showed in the face of an incredibly challenging year. At just twenty-five years of age, the popstar had known more success and tragedy than a woman her age should have. She alluded to that very idea during her acceptance speech as she reflected candidly: "This has been one of the best years of my career and the worst of my life." With those words, she reminded the world that power doesn't always come from perfection but from perseverance. Her Woman of the Year title wasn't just about music. It was about being a symbol of grace, survival, and unapologetic self-expression.

The "thank u, next" album dropped on February 8, 2019, just six months after the release of *Sweetener*, marking it the shortest gap between albums in her career. Despite this proximity in timeline, the two records couldn't have been more different: where *Sweetener* was sunshine after the storm, *thank u, next* was the late-night confessional, offering fans a refreshingly raw insight into the mind of their favourite popstar.

MAIN IMAGE: Ariana brings the stage to life during the opening night of the Sweetener World Tour in Albany, New York, 2019

Ariana Grande delivers a captivating performance during her headlining set at Lollapalooza music festival in Chicago, Illinois, 2019

Stellar Singles

7 rings

Released as the album's second single in January 2019, the track is a bold celebration of wealth, friendship, and female empowerment. Inspired by a real-life shopping spree Ariana had at Tiffany & Co. where she bought matching diamond rings for six of her closest friends (hence the title name), the song cleverly flips the narrative of heartbreak on its head. Instead of wallowing, Ariana reclaims her agency, flaunting her independence and success through luxurious, trap-infused production. Built around an interpolation of "My Favourite Things" from *The Sound of Music*, "7 rings" cleverly juxtaposes classic musical theatre with modern hip hop, creating a unique but addictive sound. While some critics praised its catchy hook and fearless energy, others accused the pop star of cultural appropriation for the song's heavy use of hip-hop aesthetics. The song was also embroiled in quite a few plagiarism claims. Despite this, commercially, it was unstoppable. "7 rings" debuted at No. 1 on the Billboard Hot 100, becoming Ariana's second chart-topper, and breaking streaming records in the process.

break up with your girlfriend, i'm bored

Serving as the final single from *thank u, next*, "break up with your girlfriend, i'm bored" is as provocative as its title suggests. The track is built on a sultry, minimalist beat, with Ariana singing from the perspective of someone who knows what she wants and isn't afraid to ask for it, even if it crosses moral lines. The chorus is catchy, the delivery is teasing, and the production is slick, all coming together to create a song that feels both flirty and mischievous.

The track samples "It Makes Me Ill" by NSYNC, which gave it a nostalgic twist for early-2000s pop fans. The music video, however, is where the song took on deeper complexity. In it, Ariana is seen seducing a guy... only to end up kissing the girlfriend who looks strikingly similar to herself. This twist added an unexpected layer of self-reflection and fluidity, sparking endless fan theories about identity, desire, and self-love.

Upon its release, *thank u, next* was met with widespread critical acclaim, solidifying Ariana's status as one of the most compelling voices in modern pop. The album scored an impressive 86 out of 100 on Metacritic, the highest rating of her career, marking a significant moment in both critical and commercial recognition. *Rolling Stone's* Rob Sheffield hailed the record as "one of the year's best pop albums so far, even in a 2019 that's already turning out to be a great one for new music," adding that it "makes you suspect the best Ariana is yet to come."

Fans echoed the critics' enthusiasm, turning the album into a cultural phenomenon. Ariana made history by becoming the first solo artist ever to occupy the top three spots on the Billboard Hot 100 simultaneously, with "7 rings" at number one, "break up with your girlfriend, i'm bored" debuting at number two, and "thank u, next" at number three. The only other act to achieve such a feat was none other than the Beatles, back in 1964. There was no longer any debate... Ariana was the biggest popstar in the world.

MAIN IMAGE: Ariana live at Lollapalooza music festival in Chicago, Illinois, 2019

Don't Call Me Angel

By the end of 2019, Ariana added yet another feather in her already impressive cap when she became an executive producer. Teaming up with music industry powerhouses Savan Kotecha and Scooter Braun, Ariana co-produced the soundtrack for the *Charlie's Angels* reboot, directed by Elizabeth Banks. In addition to lending her curatorial ear behind the scenes, Ariana also lent her voice to the lead single off the movie soundtrack, entitled "Don't Call Me Angel", featuring two more pop powerhouses Miley Cyrus and Lana Del Rey. The genre-blending track quickly gained attention for its unexpected pairing and moody, empowering energy. As co-producer, Ariana helped craft a vibe that was bold, feminine, and fierce, mirroring the spirit of the *Charlie's Angels* franchise, further cementing her reputation not just as a pop star, but as a formidable force in the music industry.

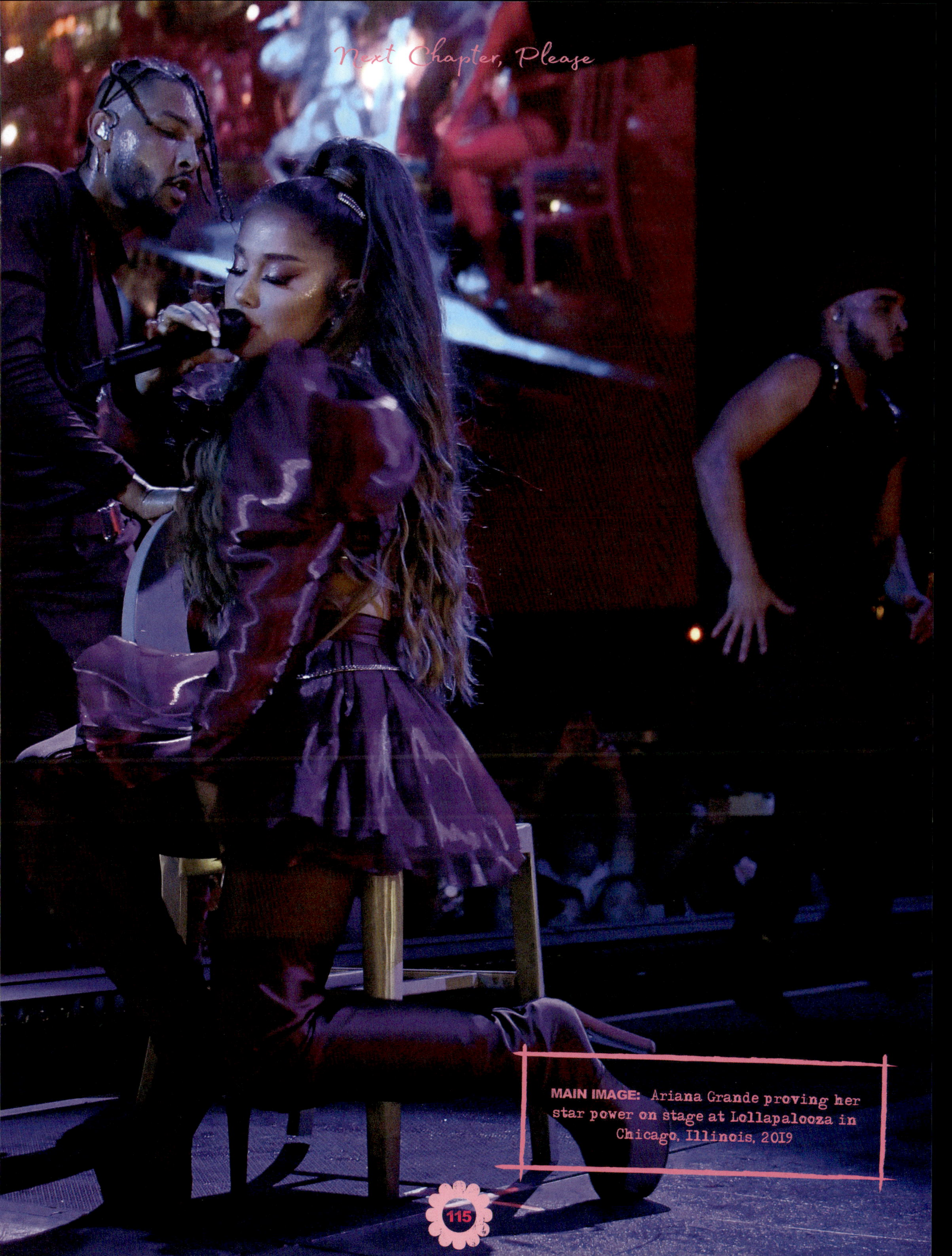

MAIN IMAGE: Ariana Grande proving her star power on stage at Lollapalooza in Chicago, Illinois, 2019

Love in Lockdown

When the world came to a standstill in 2020, most people took the opportunity to slow down, reflect, and rest. But for Ariana, rest wasn't part of the plan. In true Ariana fashion, she used the moment not just to create, but to give back. As the COVID-19 pandemic sent shockwaves around the globe, Ariana joined forces with fellow pop artist Justin Bieber for a heartfelt collaboration titled "Stuck with U", released on May 8, 2020. The track not only served as a romantic quarantine anthem but as a charitable initiative, with all net proceeds from its sales donated to the First Responders Children's Foundation, to help support families of frontline workers affected by the pandemic.

MAIN IMAGE: Ariana captured at the 62nd Annual Grammy Awards in Los Angeles, California, in 2020

Stuck with U

Musically, "Stuck with U" is a stripped-down, sweet ballad that perfectly captured the strange mix of intimacy and isolation that defined the early days of lockdown. Its accompanying music video, stitched together from home videos submitted by fans and celebrities alike, painted a warm, tender picture of what it meant to be "stuck" with someone you love. From everyday couples dancing in their living rooms to stars like Kendall Jenner, Gwyneth Paltrow, and Stephen and Ayesha Curry sharing glimpses of their quarantined lives, the video was well and truly a time capsule. But it was the final few seconds of the video that had fans buzzing. The singer, dressed in cosy loungewear, stands up and kisses a tall, dark-haired man whose face is mostly hidden from view. That mysterious moment served as a soft launch for her relationship with real estate agent Dalton Gomez, a romance that had quietly bloomed in private before being publicly confirmed with that subtle but significant kiss.

"Stuck with U" debuted at number one on the Billboard Hot 100, becoming Ariana's third chart-topping single and solidifying her place as one of the defining voices of the moment. The achievement also tied her with Mariah Carey and Drake for the most songs to debut at number one—a testament to her enduring popularity and cultural relevance even in the most uncertain of times.

ABOVE: Cover of her sixth album Positions

RIGHT: Ariana performing during the 2020 MTV Video Music Awards, broadcast on August 30, 2020

While her heart was full, so was her creative spirit. On October 30, 2020, Ariana released her sixth studio album, *Positions*, a sultry, sonically cohesive project that saw her step fully into a new, more stable chapter of her life. Lyrically, *Positions* explored themes of domesticity, intimacy, emotional security, and sexual agency. Rather than shouting her independence, Ariana whispered it, inviting listeners into the mundane of her day to day. Critics praised the album for its consistency, cohesiveness, and its subtle, elegant exploration of adult themes.

Stellar Singles

positions

The eponymous lead single, "positions" marked a shift in Ariana's narrative. It wasn't just about romantic love, but about the expectation placed on women to be able to juggle a career, intimacy and domestic chores. The music video mirrored this balance perfectly, showing Ariana as a fictional U.S. President who seamlessly transitions between high-powered meetings and domestic bliss in the kitchen. It was a cheeky but meaningful statement: women can hold it down in every room they walk into.

34-35

With its eyebrow-raising title, "34+35" quickly became one of the most talked-about songs on the album. The upbeat, playful track fused sparkling pop production with tongue-in-cheek lyrics, showcasing Ariana's comfort in expressing her sexuality without shame or apology. Though critics were divided, some calling it empowering, others finding it overtly sexual, the song was undeniably catchy. The song quickly went viral on TikTok and charted globally, becoming a fan favourite for its playful energy. In January 2021, Ariana doubled down on the track's popularity by releasing a remix featuring Doja Cat and Megan Thee Stallion. The remix injected even more heat into the song, with both rappers delivering fiery, witty verses that elevated the track from bedroom bop to full-blown power anthem. The remix propelled "34+35" to even greater chart success, eventually peaking at No. 2 on the Billboard Hot 100, and solidifying it as one of the defining songs of the *Positions* era.

pov

Arguably the emotional heart of the album, "pov" (short for "point of view") strips away the sass and confidence to reveal a more vulnerable Ariana. The track explores the idea of seeing oneself through a lover's eyes, someone who sees only beauty, strength, and grace. With soft instrumentation and deeply emotive vocals, "pov" quickly became a fan favourite and a testament to Ariana's growth, both as a lyricist and as a woman learning to love herself.

Commercially, the album was another triumph for Ariana—debuting at number one on the Billboard 200 and spawning multiple hit singles. With its blend of sultry ballads, flirtatious pop, and emotionally resonant tracks, *Positions* painted the picture of an artist in love and unapologetically embracing every facet of her womanhood. And with all the loved-up, and sometimes risqué, lyrics scattered throughout the record, fans were eager to know more about the man who had clearly inspired the pop princess.

Music, Romance and Headlines

Ariana and Dalton reportedly began dating in January 2020 but were first publicly spotted in March. Wanting to avoid another high-profile relationship, Ariana decided to keep things low-key according to insiders, making it quite the departure from her previous whirlwind romance with ex-fiancé Pete Davidson.

The couple then quarantined together during the peak of the pandemic, splitting time between Ariana's homes in Los Angeles and New York. It was in those quieter, more intimate months that she realized he was very special and by the summer, she had officially moved in with him in her newly purchased Hollywood Hills home. Dalton, unlike many of Ariana's previous partners, comes from outside the entertainment world and actually works as a luxury estate realtor. Interestingly, it was through real estate that he and Ariana first crossed paths. Her team had hired him to help find a getaway property, and upon their first meeting, the singer immediately thought he was cute. The rest, as they say, is history.

Their relationship moved quickly but felt grounded. On December 20, 2020, Ariana announced their engagement with a simple Instagram post captioned "Forever n then some," featuring a pearl-and-diamond ring. The couple married just five months later on May 15, 2021, in an ultra-private ceremony at her Montecito home with fewer than 20 guests in attendance.

r.e.m beauty

In November 2021, Ariana expanded her creative empire with the launch of r.e.m. beauty, a cosmetic brand inspired by her song "R.E.M." from the *Sweetener* album. The brand embodies Ariana's vision of makeup as a tool for self-expression, offering vegan and cruelty-free products that blend futuristic aesthetics with innovative formulas. The brand's packaging caused quite a stir among the internet as it draws inspiration from vintage space-age design, featuring sleek, silver, rounded components reminiscent of props from *Star Trek* or *Black Mirror.* This design choice reflects Ariana's fascination with sci-fi and her desire to create a unique, otherworldly experience for users. Notably, the brand's Sweetener Foundation line offers an inclusive range of 60 shades, catering to diverse skin tones. Following its successful launch, r.e.m. beauty quickly expanded its retail footprint, landing on the shelves of Ulta Beauty stores across the U.S. by March 2022. The brand's presence proved to be a hit with consumers, and according to *Forbes*, it played a significant role in boosting Ulta's gross margin—thanks to strong and consistent customer demand. As of 2025, r.e.m Beauty is valued at over US$500 million, proving that anything Ariana touches turns to gold.

Even with a wedding, an album release and global beauty empire under her belt, Ariana wasn't done. At the end of 2021, the pop star made her long-awaited return to acting with a cameo in the star-studded Netflix satire *Don't Look Up*, directed by Adam McKay. The film follows two low-level astronomers, Dr. Randall Mindy (Leonardo DiCaprio) and Kate Dibiasky (Jennifer Lawrence) who discover a massive comet hurtling toward Earth. With just six months to prevent total annihilation, they embark on a desperate media tour to warn the public. However, their warnings are met with apathy, political spin, and viral distraction, as the world becomes more obsessed with celebrity gossip than imminent doom. Ariana shines in her portrayal of pop star Riley Bina, whose over-the-top breakup and reconciliation with rapper DJ Chello (Kid Cudi) becomes a bigger news story than the end of the world. The film offers a biting critique of misinformation, government incompetence, and the prioritization of spectacle over science.

Ariana's performance, both comedic and vocal, was met with praise and proved that her acting chops were still as sharp as ever... this will come into play as she enters the next and most important phase of her career to date.

MAIN IMAGE: Ariana performing in Don't Look Up, 2021

Rewind. Erase. Repeat.

After stepping away from the music scene to focus on her acting career, Ariana Grande stunned fans by returning with an album she never intended to make. In January 2024, three years after *Positions*, she re-emerged with the lead single from what would become the most personal and emotionally raw record of her career: *eternal sunshine*. The album arrived just weeks before news of her divorce from Dalton Gomez became public, though the pair had quietly separated nearly a year earlier, on February 20, 2023. While the split had remained largely private, fans didn't need confirmation—the music made it heartbreakingly clear.

In a revealing interview with Zach Sang, Ariana confessed that she hadn't planned to release another album until 2027. But as life unravelled in unexpected ways, as it often does, so too did her creative process. Propelled by emotional upheaval, personal growth, and the unravelling of her marriage, she began writing again. The result was *eternal sunshine*, a cinematic, genre-blurring exploration of heartache, introspection, and resilience. Named after one of her favourite films, *Eternal Sunshine of the Spotless Mind*, the album plays like a soundtrack to emotional rebirth, with Ariana guiding listeners through the delicate dance of remembering, releasing, and starting again.

MAIN IMAGE: Ariana at the 62nd Annual Grammy Awards on January 26, 2020, in Los Angeles, California

2024
PART
ONE

Love, Loss & Memory

Released in 2004, *Eternal Sunshine of the Spotless Mind* is a genre-defying romantic sci-fi drama directed by Michel Gondry and written by Charlie Kaufman. The film stars none other than Ariana's childhood crush, Jim Carrey, and Kate Winslet as Joel and Clementine, a former couple who, after a painful breakup, each undergo a procedure to erase the other from their memories. But as Joel relives their relationship in reverse during the erasure process, he begins to realize that he doesn't want to forget. What unfolds is a poignant, visually inventive meditation on love, loss, memory, and the pain and beauty of emotional vulnerability.

The film struck a deep chord with many, including Ariana who has long cited *Eternal Sunshine* as one of her all-time favourite movies. It's no surprise, then, that she chose to title her seventh studio album in homage to the film. Much like the movie, Ariana's album grapples with themes of heartbreak, healing, and the desire to hold on to what once was—even when letting go might be the only way forward.

Yet unlike a traditional breakup album, *eternal sunshine* doesn't wallow. It's cathartic, elegant, and healing. It's decidedly not a revenge album but rather a reckoning.

MAIN IMAGE: Ariana performs at the 2024 Met Gala, celebrating Sleeping Beauties: Reawakening Fashion, at The Metropolitan Museum of Art in New York City

LEFT: One of the cover artworks for eternal sunshine

eternal sunshine debuted at number one on the Billboard 200, marking Ariana's sixth album to top the chart. The album received widespread acclaim, with critics praising its narrative cohesion, lyrical vulnerability, and sonic elegance. *Pitchfork* described it as "Ariana's most emotionally honest record yet, balancing wistfulness with clarity" and *Rolling Stone* called it "a masterclass in post-heartbreak storytelling".

With *eternal sunshine,* Ariana Grande didn't just return to music; she redefined it on her terms. No longer chasing the high of chart-topping success, she embraced subtlety, storytelling, and self-reflection. This album wasn't about radio hits or viral TikToks—it was about healing. And in doing so, Ariana proved once again that her power as an artist lies not only in her voice, but in her vulnerability.

The 2024 Met Gala at The Metropolitan Museum of Art, New York City

Stellar Singles

yes, and?

Released as the lead single off *eternal sunshine*, the track marked a sonic departure from her previous soft, sultry ballads, she had become known for. With its infectious energy, spoken-word sass, and throwback synths, many listeners drew immediate comparisons to Madonna's "Vogue", both in sound and in spirit. Lyrically, "yes, and?" is about confronting criticism with grace and self-assurance. It also felt like Ariana's answer to all the noise surrounding her personal life. The accompanying music video leaned heavily into musical theatre aesthetics, with choreography and styling reminiscent of *Fame* or *A Chorus Line*, nodding to Ariana's theatre-kid roots. Commercially, the song was a triumph. "yes, and?" debuted at number one on the Billboard Hot 100, becoming Ariana's eighth chart-topping single and reaffirming her place as a pop powerhouse unbothered by public speculation and ready to tell her story on her own terms.

we can't be friends (wait for your love)

"we can't be friends (wait for your love)" stands as one of the emotional high points of *eternal sunshine*, offering listeners a stripped-back, vulnerable ballad that dives deep into the complexities of heartbreak and boundaries. The song finds Ariana grappling with the painful realization that love doesn't always survive in the aftermath of a breakup and that sometimes, the healthiest choice is to walk away completely, no matter how strong the connection once was. With haunting synths, minimal percussion, and echoing vocals, the track has a melancholic, dreamlike quality, reminiscent of Robyn's "Dancing On My Own" but softer and more introspective. Lyrically, it's mature and self-aware: Ariana doesn't place blame, but rather acknowledges the emotional cost of trying to stay friends with someone she still loves. The accompanying music video, cinematic and surreal, was styled like a retro-futuristic sci-fi short film, further reinforcing the *Eternal Sunshine of the Spotless Mind* influence throughout the album. Upon release, "we can't be friends" debuted at number one on the Billboard Hot 100, marking another chart-topping achievement for Grande and securing the track as a fan and critical favourite alike.

the boy is mine

In a twist of tone, "the boy is mine" is Ariana's fantasy villain era. Inspired by the 1998 Brandy & Monica hit of the same name, the track is sultry, theatrical, and a little unhinged in the best way. Featuring hypnotic melodies and a seductive beat, Ariana plays the role of the unapologetic anti-hero who owns her desire, even if it's morally grey. In the music video, Ariana portrays a Catwoman-inspired character who becomes infatuated with Mayor Max Starling, played by Penn Badgley. Ariana decides to concoct a love potion and infiltrate the mayor's apartment with the intention of winning his affection. However, upon confronting him, she discovers that the potion is unnecessary, as he is already enamoured with her. The video features cameo appearances by Brandy and Monica as news anchors, adding a nostalgic touch to the modern reinterpretation. It's cheeky, dark, and unforgettable.

LEFT AND ABOVE: Brandy & Monica, 1999 and the cover of the original song of the same title

Welcome to Oz

In the same year, Ariana went from topping the charts with her brand-new album, *eternal sunshine,* to starring in one of the biggest box office successes of the year: *Wicked.* For Ariana, this wasn't just another role but the fulfilment of a lifelong dream. Since her teenage years, the pop star had openly expressed her desire to play Glinda the Good Witch, citing *Wicked* as one of her favourite ever musicals. In various interviews over the past decade, the singer has gushed about her love for the Broadway hit and even tweeted lyrics from the show long before she ever stepped into Glinda's heels. So, when it was announced that she would star in the film adaptation of *Wicked,* alongside Cynthia Erivo as Elphaba, it felt less like a casting decision and more like destiny.

Based on Gregory Maguire's 1995 novel *Wicked: The Life and Times of the Wicked Witch of the West* and adapted from the beloved Broadway musical of the same name, *Wicked* offers a reimagined origin story of the witches of Oz, long before Dorothy dropped in. The story follows Elphaba, a misunderstood young woman born with green skin, and her unlikely friendship with the bubbly and ambitious Glinda. As the two navigate magic school, social hierarchies, and their clashing beliefs, their bond is tested by love, politics, and the pressures of a society quick to label what it doesn't understand. With themes of identity, prejudice, and the blurry line between good and evil, the two-part film, directed by Jon M. Chu (of Crazy Rich Asians and In the Heights fame), promises to take all the best aspects of the original production, and turn it into a massive cinematic spectacle.

Much like the viral "Barbenheimer" (Barbie and Oppenheimer) phenomenon of 2023, the release of *Wicked (Part One)* alongside *Gladiator II* on the same weekend in 2024 sparked a fan-made crossover dubbed "Glicked". What began as a tongue-in-cheek internet joke quickly exploded into a full-blown cultural event, with fans dressing up for double features, creating memes, mashups, and themed content celebrating the cinematic clash. The *Wicked* press tour, as a result, became just as much a spectacle as the film itself, full of viral interviews, dramatic fashion, and emotional moments. This wasn't just a press junket, but a cultural moment.

RIGHT: Promotional shot for Wicked

2024
PART
TWO

A Wicked (Press) Tour

Method Dressing

Throughout the *Wicked* press tour, Ariana Grande and Cynthia Erivo took "method dressing" to dazzling new heights, fully embracing their on-screen personas of Glinda and Elphaba. Rather than treating the red carpet as a traditional promotional stop, the duo leaned into a theatrical, immersive aesthetic that blurred the lines between costume and couture. Ariana consistently appeared in pastel pinks, voluminous gowns, sparkles, and opera gloves, channeling Glinda's bubbly elegance with a high-fashion twist, while Cynthia arrived in deep emeralds, structured silhouettes, and dramatic capes, a sartorial nod to Elphaba's strength and mystery. The commitment didn't go unnoticed by fans, who dubbed the duo's looks as "Wicked-core" and praised the fashion-forward homage to their characters.

Poster Controversy

One of the more surprising flashpoints of the *Wicked* press tour came in October 2024, when the official character poster featuring Cynthia Erivo and Ariana Grande—recreating the original Broadway art—was released to mark the film's ticket sales launch. The response was mixed. While some fans embraced the stylised homage, others took to social media with their own "fan edits," using Photoshop and AI tools to recreate a poster that more closely resembled the iconic original, complete with obscured eyes, a smirk, and a raised hand. One such edit, which aimed to bring back Elphaba's signature red lips and hidden gaze, quickly went viral. But instead of praise, it sparked outrage. Cynthia Erivo publicly responded via Instagram, calling the edit "the wildest, most offensive thing" she had seen, saying it "degrades me" and "degrades us." She emphasized that the new poster was meant as an homage, not a copy, and that obscuring her face felt like an erasure of her performance. While the fan behind the edit deleted it out of respect, they later reinstated the image, stating their intentions were never malicious. Ariana Grande weighed in diplomatically, calling it "a massive adjustment period" as audiences and creators navigate the ethics of fan art and AI editing. Erivo later reflected on the situation with more nuance, describing her response as "a human moment" of wanting to protect the character of Elphaba.

MAIN IMAGE: Wicked promotional shot featured on theatre posters, paying homage to the original stage poster

Merchandise Mishap

One of the most unexpected controversies to emerge from the *Wicked* marketing blitz came not from the film itself, but from the toy aisle. In a partnership with Mattel, a series of official *Wicked* dolls were released, featuring characters like Glinda, Elphaba, Fiyero, Madame Morrible. However, the rollout was quickly overshadowed by a major oversight. In November 2024, consumers discovered that the doll packaging and accompanying manuals mistakenly listed the website, which directed users to an adult film site operated by Wicked Pictures, rather than the intended www.wickedmovie.com. The error caused significant backlash, particularly among parents, prompting Mattel to issue an immediate apology and urge customers to destroy any affected packaging. To add to the chaos, earlier in August, sound chips embedded in Mattel's singing dolls had already leaked snippets of songs from the film like "Popular" and "Defying Gravity", effectively spoiling key moments ahead of the official soundtrack release. What was meant to be a celebratory merchandising tie-in had instead become a PR nightmare.

Holding Space

Among the many viral moments, none garnered quite as much internet buzz as Cynthia Erivo's emotional reaction to a reporter. During an interview with *Out* magazine's Tracy E. Gilchrist, the reporter referenced how fans had connected deeply with the film's closing number "Defying Gravity," saying that people were "taking the lyrics and really holding space with that." Cynthia, visibly moved, placed her hand on her chest and appeared to hold back tears, responding, "I didn't know that was happening... that's really powerful. That's what I wanted." While the sentiment was genuine, social media quickly latched onto the moment, turning it into a meme. Seeing her co-star start to get emotional, Ariana showed support by delicately grabbing Cynthia's index finger, an oddly tender gesture that only fuelled the meme's staying power. The "holding space" moment became emblematic of the tour's overall tone as it was dramatic, deeply felt, and unintentionally a little weird.

LEFT: Cynthia Erivo and Ariana Grande at the Los Angeles premiere of *Wicked* in November, 2024

ABOVE: Mattel's *Wicked* dolls

Music, Romance and Headlines

Ethan Slater

While filming *Wicked*, Ariana's off-screen life once again made headlines but this time for her relationship with co-star Ethan Slater, who plays Boq in the film. Slater wasn't new to the spotlight. He rose to fame for his critically acclaimed performance as SpongeBob SquarePants in the Broadway musical adaptation, earning a Tony Award nomination and a reputation as one of theatre's most exciting young talents. News of their romance broke in July 2023, just days after Ariana's split from husband Dalton Gomez became public. The timing sparked immediate backlash, particularly as Slater was reportedly still legally married to singer and high school sweetheart Lilly Jay, with whom he shares a young child. Social media quickly erupted, many accusing Ariana of being a "homewrecker," a label she has been unfairly branded with in the past. The story snowballed into a tabloid frenzy, with Slater's estranged wife giving a rare public statement to Page Six, claiming, "My family is just collateral damage". Sources close to the couple insisted that both Ariana and Ethan were already separated from their respective partners before beginning their relationship. Still, the scandal refused to die down, and Ariana once again found herself at the centre of a media storm. It was rumoured that the studio suggested the couple keep a low profile for a couple of months, to make sure their messy relationship drama doesn't affect the success of the movie. Since the release of *Wicked*, the couple have been spotted in restaurants and award ceremonies but neither has directly addressed the cheating allegations.

TOP RIGHT: Ariana and Ethan attend the 97th Annual Oscars in Hollywood, California, in March, 2025

Wicked flew into cinemas with sky-high expectations—and managed to exceed them. Upon its release, the film was met with widespread acclaim from both critics and audiences alike. Praise was heaped on its lavish visuals, sweeping musical numbers, and the powerhouse performances of its leads. The film opened to a record-breaking $114 million at the U.S. box office, making it the highest-grossing debut for a musical adaptation in history, and soared to $164 million globally in its first weekend. Critics celebrated *Wicked* as a bold, emotionally rich blockbuster that brought the beloved stage production to life in a way that was both nostalgic and refreshingly modern.

The Afterglow

Following the whirlwind success of *Wicked*, Ariana has continued to explore her creative passions, delving deeper into both music and film. In March 2025, she released *eternal sunshine deluxe: brighter days ahead*, a reissue of her acclaimed seventh studio album, with an additional six new tracks. As part of the release campaign, the deluxe version of the album was accompanied by a short film of the same name. Co-written and co-directed by Grande, the 26-minute sci-fi drama marked her directorial debut and expanded upon the narrative introduced in her "we can't be friends (wait for your love)" music video. The film, featuring Grande reprising her Catwoman-inspired role, offered fans a poignant, futuristic meditation on memory and loss.

Despite the album's success, the singer has confirmed that she will not embark on a tour in 2025. Earlier discussions of a "mini-tour" between the two *Wicked* films were ultimately shelved due to her demanding schedule and a renewed focus on acting. In interviews, she has expressed a desire to prioritized her theatrical roots, stating that while music remains a vital part of her life, she intends to slow down her pop music output to concentrate on roles that allow her to explore different facets of her artistry.

Looking ahead, Ariana is set to reprise her role as Glinda in *Wicked: Part Two*, scheduled for release in November 2025. She has already begun promotional activities for the sequel, including a presentation at CinemaCon in April 2025, where she and co-star Cynthia Erivo teased new footage and promised a more restrained press tour. As she continues to balance her multifaceted career, Ariana remains committed to evolving as an artist, embracing new challenges while staying connected to her musical origins.

MAIN IMAGE: Ariana at the 62nd Annual Grammy Awards in Los Angeles, California in January, 2020

2025